Dedric D. Perry's Playbook

A Book of Wisdom Nuggets and Simple Strategies for Life
Volume 1

DEDRIC D. PERRY

Dedric D. Perry's Playbook

Published by Marc Britt Media and Publishing

Copyright © 2018 Dedric D. Perry

Cover design by Brittany Murray of Marc Britt Media and Publishing © 2018. Photography by Reggie Anderson © 2018. Scripture quotations are from the Hebrew- Greek Key Word Study Bible; YouVersion Bible App, kingjamesbibleonline.org; knowing-jesus.com; dailyverses.net; biblegateway.com; dictionary.com; *New King James Version of the Holy Bible*, Copyright © 1982 by Thomas Nelson. Used by permission. All rights reserved.

ISBN-10: 1725590352
ISBN-13: 978-1725590359

DEDICATION

I would like to dedicate this literary work to The Lord Jesus Christ, our Father; to my loving family, my spiritual leaders, my church family and my spiritual sons and daughters who has been my greatest supports and *"the wind beneath my wing."* You all have been my eyes and listening ears throughout the years and have been with me through thick and thin! I am truly grateful for you all!

I would also like to dedicate this work to Pastor Harold Wilder, who was one of the greatest prophets to walk the earth but has since, gone home to be with the Lord. You were the first pastor that spoke into my life, activated, and cultivated the gifts within me and showed me who I was in God. I am so truly grateful to God for you! Continue to rest in Heaven and rest in peace! You will never be forgotten and will always be remembered and missed!

CONTENTS

ACKNOWLEDGMENTS

I would like to give a special acknowledgement to my husband, Sgt. Anthony Perry, who is my earthly lord, headship, covering, protector, lover, confidant and companion. Truly it is who you are and all that you do that makes it easy for me to do what I do! I truly love, appreciate, and thank you for all of your love, sacrifice, wisdom, support and encouragement. You are truly the greatest husband, lover and friend that God could have blessed me with.

To my mom, Elder Hazel Hyman, who gave birth to me. I honor you! It is because of you that I am the woman and woman of God that I am today! You have truly been my rock, my wisdom, my confidant and a true encouragement to me. I appreciate you for all that you do! Thank you for all of your love, sacrifice, support and encouragement.

To my dad, Clinton Weatherbee. It is because of you that I am here today! You have been a blessing to me more than you know and a great inspiration to me. I thank you and appreciate you for being you, and a true encouragement. Thank you for all of the things you have taught me that you may not have realized. I have learned more from you than you would ever know. Thank you for all of your love, support and encouragement.

To my daughter, Minister India Hyman, and my two beautiful grandchildren, Jaylen and Kayleh. You all are "my loves," my joy, my inspiration, my rock, my pillars, and encouragement. It is because of you, "my loves," that I do what I do. You all have been there for me more than you would know. Thank you all for your love, sacrifice, support and encouragement.

To my spiritual leaders, Bishop Dr. Bonnie Hunter and Apostle Barbara Stewart James, you both are spiritual mothers to me who have covered, undergirded, nurtured, cultivated and equipped me in ministry and have greatly poured into my life spiritually. I am truly grateful and appreciative for all that the both of you have done for me, and for the life of Abundant Reign Ministry, Inc. and DDP Ministries. Thank you all for your love, counsel, wisdom, encouragement and support.

To my church family, "Abundant Reign Ministry," to my spiritual sons and daughters, to my covenant brothers and sisters, and to all who have been there for me on this journey! You all have poured into my life tremendously in your own way, and have encouraged, inspired, supported and believed in me throughout the years. I greatly appreciate you all and am truly grateful to God for you.

God bless and I love you all!

WORDS FROM MY HUSBAND

Dedric has a very selfless personality. She loves hard and feels deeply for people, and I believe that this drives her passion to save souls. She has a great ability to process a situation or something that may seem complicated, and reduce it into simpler terms that are enlightening, while simultaneously bringing clarity that can only be defined as wisdom of divine origin, rather than a ubiquitous nature. Her personality of magnanimity allows her audience to gravitate towards her with great ease. Her humility never transforms into vanity because her love for humanity absconds the mere thought of it. She is genuinely only interested in the uplifting of God's purpose and His will; if you ever hear her speak, it becomes obviously clear that she is a vessel and messenger of truth.

Sgt. Anthony F. Perry

WORDS FROM MY BISHOP

Apostle Dedric Perry has walked this journey of Christendom for a long time; in that time she has experienced life as a Christian, and has gained knowledge and wisdom from God. God has certainly poured out wisdom into her life and now she is pouring it out to others through teaching and preaching the Word of God with revelation. Her wisdom acts properly upon that knowledge, speaking boldly and letting people know of their consequences whether good or bad if they do or do not adhere to it. She teaches with such accuracy, while helping individuals to recognize the right course of action and inspiring them to have the will and courage to follow it. Dedric has the "know how" to apply wisdom in any given situation. As she delivers the Word of God through teaching and preaching, sound wisdom comes forth, discerning what is true and right. God has given her the ability to teach principles with wisdom where even a child can understand. Dedric speaks to individuals in simple language to give them wisdom in their walk through life circumstances. She is so profound in her delivery that it causes you to give an ear to hear because when she speaks, it is God that uses her to speak to the core issues that affect people's lives. People's lives are changed just sitting under her tutoring. Dedric teaches with the wisdom from above that is easily to be entreated. She is truly a Woman of Wisdom!

Dr. Bonnie Hunter

INTRODUCTION

Dedric D. Perry's Playbook is a book of wisdom that has been indebted through my life experiences. Some of the greatest lessons I've learned in life were through life itself. In life, I have learned to value the lessons and experiences, and have allowed them to personally speak to me. These lessons coupled with God's Word became principles and wisdom nuggets for me as the Lord continued to reveal great things concerning them. As a result, I have been able to LIVE my LIFE by them successfully and victoriously.

These lessons did not only serve as principles and wisdom nuggets, but also as simple strategies for everyday living! They became strategies that I used daily in my life, which for me, resulted in effective living!

My life experiences also taught me the practicality of life. God then began speaking to me in regards to the *"simplicity of life,"* which later spilled over into my ministry life, hence the concept of this book. This book was derived through a revelation given to me by The Lord saying, "Simplicity is key in delivery to ensure comprehension of the mystery; it is vital and essential." God also guided me to Psalms 119:130 which states, "The entrance of your Words gives light, it gives understanding to the simple." At that point, I also began to minister with a more simplistic approach. The Lord began to reveal and say to me, "it's not always that people don't want to receive my words or are outright rebelling and defying My Word. Sometimes they just don't understand and I need someone to give them something that they can understand."

Certainly, everyone still won't understand for more reasons than one, but at least they have a chance! He begin to remind me that everyone has a different level of comprehension and I had to be mindful of that! It's not always that they *don't* get it but sometimes they *can't* get it! The Lord then placed a burden on my heart for those who just don't understand and gave me a strategy on how to incorporate them as well; not because they weren't deep, spiritual enough or super spooky, but in some cases the message isn't relatable enough. For some people, they just can't comprehend because it oftentimes go over their heads, and need the message to be brought to a level that they can understand. This could be very challenging in delivery for those of us who flow in revelatory knowledge! How do you deliver the revelation without losing the people? Remember, even Jesus had to explain some of His teachings. He had to give the people something they could understand to bring them to His understanding. Jesus spoke in parables *"a simple story used to illustrate a moral or spiritual lesson"* that can also be defined as *"an earthly story with a heavenly meaning."* Jesus had to give them an earthly interpretation of a spiritual revelation! Although some of His parables were intended to hide things from those who didn't believe, it opened up things for those who did believe! He used parables as parallels; comparisons between what they could understand and what He wanted them to understand.

As God began to change my approach and delivery style, I was able to reach a mixed multitude. Whether you were on a collegiate, elementary, middle or high school level, or even if you had a learning disability, you would be able to understand! My grandson who is nine years old repeats back to me what he has learned from my teachings with clarity and understanding, which brings me much joy in knowing that even he can understand. Sometimes we can make things so deep and complicated that we miss the simple things in life. When looking for something deeper, we oftentimes miss what's right before us. More often than not, the answers are hidden in plain sight. We have become so fascinated with deepness that we have overlooked the simplistic. When searching for the deeper things of God, as we should, we sometimes miss some of the simple things that God is trying to show us in life. A well balanced life is a LIFE that's properly LIVED.

Over the years, I've learned that life is a phenomenal teacher once lessons are learned and applied! What I have realized is that each experience and lesson is designed to be "clues in life" that leads us to the next place in life. God's wisdom and revelatory knowledge was the compass to guide me through each clue, and as a result, this helped me to navigate through life and learn life. Sometimes we just have to learn life. We have to learn life in order to LIVE LIFE and to properly maneuver through it. I was able to learn from the lessons that I received in life and those "life lessons" showed me what to do or not to do with the rest of my life. Sometimes we just have to learn the lessons in order to learn life.

Please know that these precepts are not law, but rather a school of thoughts and revealed knowledge given to me by God, based off of His

Word applied throughout the course of my life. I would like to share with you what God has shared with me. I believe that if these principles, wisdom nuggets, and strategies work for me, then they can work for you too. I know that these principles will work, as long as you work them.

My life experiences have taught me so much, but the greatest of them is how to "LIVE LIFE and stop letting LIFE LIVE you." It has also taught me how to "stop existing and LIVE in order to fulfill." Both of these mantras have become my motto in life. Actually, there is a "LIVE LIFE" chapter in this book, as well as *Stop Letting* and *I'm Convinced,* which was birthed through things that I had to personally stop letting people to do me, and things that I am convinced about after experiencing, witnessing, and observing some of the same things over and over again. So, enjoy! I pray that this book is a tremendous blessing to you and that it will provide much wisdom, insight, inspiration, illumination, enlightenment, and encouragement!

Remember, we cannot fulfill LIFE until we LIVE LIFE!

1 LIVE LIFE

There'll be two dates on your tombstone and all your friends will read 'em but all that's gonna matter is that little dash between 'em.

-Kevin Welch-

Twenty years from now you will be more disappointed by the things you didn't do than by the things you did.

-Mark Twain-

You only live once, but if you do it right, once is enough.

-Joe Lewis-

The purpose of life, after all, is to live it, to taste experience to the utmost, to reach out eagerly and without fear for newer and richer experience.

-Eleanor Roosevelt-

Imagination is everything. It is the preview of life's coming attraction.

-Albert Einstein-

Always remember that "Life should be Lived".

-Anonymous-

LIVE LIFE and STOP letting LIFE LIVE you!

No longer *EXIST* but LIVE!

Stop *EXISTING* and LIVE! You have to LIVE to FULFILL!

We have to MOVE from just *EXISTING* to LIVING into FULFILLING!

We cannot FULFILL until we LIVE!

We must LIVE LIFE INTENTIONALLY!

LIVE LIFE on PURPOSE!

LIVE the LIFE GOD INTENDED you to LIVE!

Let LIFE LIVE for you instead of LIFE LIVING you!

Let LIFE WORK for you instead of WORKING you!

GET UP and LIVE LIFE the way you were PURPOSED to!

LIVE LIFE on PURPOSE in order to LIVE IT with PURPOSE!

The WAY we VIEW LIFE is the WAY we LIVE LIFE!

When we change our VIEW on LIFE, our VIEW will change our LIFE!

In order to LIVE LIFE VICTORIOUSLY you have to leave *EXISTING* behind you to embrace the LIFE before you!

It is important to know that we *ALL* have a PURPOSE in LIFE but it's difficult to FIND what we didn't realize needed to be FOUND!

You say *"I DON'T"* know what my PURPOSE is and I say *"YES you DO"* it's wherever your PASSION is!

Our PURPOSE is HIDDEN in our PASSION! FIND your PASSION you'll FIND your PURPOSE!

Your PASSION + your PURPOSE = your DESTINY!

Sometimes the reason we don't know our PURPOSE in LIFE is because we're consumed with LIFE! It doesn't give us time to take time to *DISCOVER or UNCOVER* our PURPOSE in LIFE because it's *COVERED* by the cares of LIFE!

You can't allow LIFE to LIVE your LIFE! It's time to *REDISCOVER* the LIFE that *GOD DISCOVERED* for you!

One of the GREATEST things you could ever *DO* in LIFE is LIVE and BE you! LIVE to BE you! #LIVEYOU

The LAST thing you want to *DO* is be a CHILD of GOD but *DON'T* LIVE a LIFE for GOD!

One of the GREATEST LESSONS in LIFE is LIFE! Allow LIFE to teach you LESSONS! Once *LIFE LESSONS* are learned and applied they now become some of our GREATEST COMMODITIES in LIFE!

When your LIFE is INTENTIONAL nothing is *DONE or HAPPENS* by CHANCE! Your *STEPS* have been INTENTIONALLY ordered by GOD! You are the INTENTIONS of GOD! It wasn't ACCIDENTAL it was INTENTIONAL! GOD was not scratching HIS head when HE created you! HE INTENDED so therefore you must INTEND to be who GOD has INTENTIONALLY created you to be!

Your DISPOSITION in LIFE is very important to your NEXT OPPORTUNITY in LIFE! A proper CHANGE in DISPOSITION could actually CHANGE your LIFE'S CONDITION and put you in a different POSITION!

It's *OK* to BALANCE your LIFE but just be careful not to BALANCE *GOD OUT* of your LIFE! We must learn how to master the BALANCING ACT without other things *LACKING!*

A well balanced LIFE is a LIVED LIFE! It is a LIFE that's properly LIVED!

You'll start experiencing RELIEF in your own LIFE once you RELEASE some people from your LIFE! *RELEASE* and be *RELIEVED!*

The PRESSURES of LIFE produce POWER in your LIFE!

God will allow *PRESSURE IN* you to bring *POWER OUT* of you! It'll cause you to move from a *LIFE of PRESSURE* to a *LIFE of POWER!*

GOD can always be FOUND no matter where you FIND yourself in LIFE; you can always FIND GOD in that same place in LIFE! He is never LOST! He's always THERE and can always be FOUND anywhere!

Some things we GO THROUGH in LIFE is simply because of the WAY we VIEW LIFE!

CHANGE your *VIEW* it'll CHANGE your LIFE!

Make sure your *REFLECTION* on LIFE brings about *PROGRESSION* in LIFE and not *DIGRESSION* due to what happened in LIFE!

DON'T let your *UP SETS* in LIFE *SET UP* the rest of your LIFE!

The PAST is just that...PAST! Although it was PRESENT at the TIME but now it has PASSED! It's the FORMER thing that came to FORM you!

The PAST was never designed to be PRESENT or FUTURE! It was ordained to produce your PRESENT and FUTURE! It is designed to be a FORMER YOU and was created to FORM YOU! Not for you to LIVE in IT but for you to produce LIFE out of IT!

GOD will use your PAST LIFE to establish your NEW LIFE! He wants to use *"THAT LIFE* for *THIS LIFE"!* Everything that you have ENCOUNTERED in LIFE was DESIGNED and PURPOSED to bring you somewhere else in LIFE!

Sometimes we just have to learn LIFE! We have to learn LIFE in order to LIVE LIFE and to properly maneuver through LIFE! #LearnToLive

Sometimes we just have to learn the LESSONS in order to learn LIFE!

We don't have to be *SATISFIED* with where we are in LIFE but we do need to be *CONTENT* with the STATE we're in! Our CONTENTMENT can CHANGE our CONDITION!

Remember this, LIFE itself is a PROCESS! You might be in a PROCESS in LIFE but you are also in a PROCESS called LIFE! It's just LIFE taking you somewhere *else* GREATER in LIFE! Yes, even with its UPS and DOWNS, it's UPSETS and SET UPS, it's still a SET UP for a STEP UP!

Oftentimes, the GREATEST area of your SUCCESS is HIDDEN in what you *DON'T* want to DO!

When we START walking in our PURPOSE we START walking in our EFFECTIVENESS!

 Your LIFE CHANGE will *CHANGE* the LIFE of someone else, and your CHANGED LIFE will *CHANGE* somebody else's LIFE!

Don't let a SEASONAL MOMENT become a MOMENT of a LIFETIME! Don't let that MOMENT in LIFE become a LIFETIME MOMENT!

Don't allow a PERIOD in TIME to become a PERIOD of a LIFETIME! It's just a PERIOD of TIME! #Period...

Your TRUTH will CHANGE your LIFE! It'll give you an EXCHANGE for CHANGE in LIFE!

Remember when there's a SHALL over your LIFE, there's a SHALL NOT in your LIFE! That *"SHALL NOT"* happen or take place because of the *"SHALL"* that's taken place!

DON'T let LIFE get in the way of YOUR LIFE! It's just LIFE!

Remember, your CIRCUMSTANCE is just for a MOMENT! Don't let that MOMENT last a LIFETIME!

GOD will give you a VISION, then LIFE will hit! Don't let LIFE mess up your VISION! Don't let LIFE mess with your VIEW! Don't let what you SEE become your SIN!

STOP letting LIFE get the *BEST* of YOU and get the *BEST* out of LIFE!

DON'T let LIFE mess up your LIFE! Let it show you how to LIVE LIFE!

Final Thoughts...

Always remember LIFE is ONE of the GREATEST LESSONS in LIFE! Allow the *LESSONS* that LIFE has taught you to *GUIDE* you! Let them become *PRINCIPLES* that you can LIVE by! Allow them to teach you how to LIVE LIFE and to STOP letting LIFE LIVE you!

MY THOUGHTS

2 WISDOM

James 1:5 | NAS

"If any of you lack wisdom, let him ask of God, that giveth to all men liberally, and upbraideth not; and it shall be given him."

Always VALUE your VALUE!

Do not allow others to DEVALUE you! You have to VALUE your own VALUE and it'll teach others how to VALUE you!

A NEW PLACE demands NEW ACCOMODATIONS! Sometimes you just have to make the *MOVE* to get something NEW!

Just because the PAST VISITS you, doesn't mean you have to REVISIT the PAST! Be PRESENT in your PRESENT and be PRESENT for your FUTURE!

Sometimes we have to REFOCUS our FOCUS because *WHAT and HOW* we LOOK at IT can determine *WHEN and WHERE* we're going with IT!

It's *okay* to READJUST to ADJUST! CHANGE is not always *EASY* but CHANGE is NECESSARY for your NEXT! It's a NECESSARY CHANGE for NEXT! CHANGE is your *NECESSARY* NEXT!

Sometimes we just have to RETHINK our THINKING!

Sometimes you have to REDISCOVER the *WHO* in you to DISCOVER the *WHO ARE* you!

Although *TRIALS* may *COME,* the most important and valuable lesson is *"HOW you COME THROUGH the TRIAL!"* It's the key to TRIUMPHANT and VICTORIOUS LIVING! Live TRIUMPHANT! Come through VICTORIOUSLY!

Don't allow your desire for ADVANCEMENT to frustrate your current CONTENTMENT!

You ASKED! God ANSWERED! Now *RECEIVE IT!*

It's not always about BEING DIFFERENT to make a DIFFERENCE! It's about BEING the DIFFERENCE which will make a DIFFERENCE! Making a DIFFERENCE makes you DIFFERENT!

Don't make GOD RE-SOLVE what HE already SOLVED! Problem SOLVED and RESOLVED! *next...*

When FAMILY no longer MATTERS! You now have a MATTER!

Don't let their PROBLEM with you become a PROBLEM for you! You are alright with you! They have a PROBLEM not you...

CONQUER your FEARS and you can CONQUER anything that FEARS you!

You have to REFUSE to be USED and REFUSE to be MISUSED!

FAITHFULNESS will always get you the *BEST* but COMPROMISE will always get you *LESS!*

Your RESPONSE and your REACTION means everything!

Get some *REST* and let God handle the *REST!*

It's not *EASY* but it's not *HARD* either! It's NOT EASY when you have to LET GO but it's NOT HARD when you LET GOD!

Don't allow the frustrations of *WAITING* turn PATIENTLY WAITING into ANXIOUSLY WAITING!

Don't confuse a GOOD MOVE as a GOD MOVE! A GOOD IDEA is not always a GOD IDEA!

If you want something *"NEW"* then you have to STOP doing the *"OLD!"*

If you want a *NEW* experience then you have to *STOP* experiencing the *OLD!* #YouExperiencedThatBefore

If you want something *"NEW"* then you have to *DO* something you've never *DONE* before or *GO* where you've never *GONE* before!

There's a TIME called NOW were we have to give our PAST a PASS! We have to let the PAST PASS!

Don't let your INITIAL response be your CONTINUAL response! Make the SHIFT! First comes *NATURAL* then comes *SPIRITUAL!* First comes you then comes the *GOD* in you! Let *GOD* respond for you!

Don't mess up your PROCESS trying to get to PROGRESS!

It's your HERE that takes you THERE!

The PROCESS is just as important as the PROGRESS! The PROCESS provides essentials and necessary ingredients for your PROGRESS! It helps you MAINTAIN your PROGRESS and helps you to REMAIN in IT!

The enemy doesn't mind us PROGRESSING because he knows we're not going to keep IT if we didn't *GO THROUGH* the proper PROCESS!

PAST SUCCESS is not indicative to FUTURE SUCCESS! Stay FOCUSED and remain *HUMBLE* in the process!

However *LONG* it takes us to GET IT is how *LONG* it's gonna take us to GET- IT! Once we grasp the understanding and realization of what GOD is DOING and desires for us to DO is when we'll receive the next of what GOD has for us!

Sometimes GOD doesn't release the NEXT because we haven't completed the LAST! Your *LAST* set of INSTRUCTIONS may connect with your *NEXT* series of BLESSINGS! There are dots that connect to our NEXT and sometimes those are the dots that we have to connect!

Don't let THINKING ahead mess up your THINKING now! Stop *OVER* THINKING it and just *THINK* about it! There's a difference in *OVER* THINKING and THINKING it *OVER!* STOP thinking OVER it and just think it *OVER!*

While waiting in the MEANTIME it can be a MEAN TIME but you DON'T have to allow your *"MEANTIME"* to become a *MEAN TIME!*

Sometimes you just have to SHAKE it OFF before it makes you GO OFF!

Beloveds! Don't LOSE your POSITION trying to get ATTENTION! Don't LOSE what you already *HAVE* trying to *GET* what GOD didn't GIVE!

Remember, it might be the SEASON but it still needs to be the TIME! Don't confuse *SEASONS* and *TIMES!* They can be interchangeable but there's also a difference! Just because it's YOUR SEASON it still needs to be YOUR TIME! Your SEASON will prepare you for your TIME! The SEASON tells you *WHAT TIME IT IS!* It starts LOOKING like something in order to TELL you something! It tells you that TIME is approaching and it's near! SO GET READY! Your TIME could finally be here!

Always remember, GOD has a *WILL* but HE also has a *TIME!* It might be the WILL of GOD but it also needs to be the TIMING of GOD!

If you don't SHIFT you might get STIFF! We have to learn to SHIFT with the SHIFT! TRANSITION may not be *EASY* but it's *HARDER* when you become STIFF and CAN'T SHIFT!

Sometimes we have to say to ourselves "I ALREADY did that BEFORE therefore I won't be doing that ANYMORE"! It'll save you a lot of TIME and will prevent you from WASTING TIME!

SILENCE is GOLDEN! BUT in some cases *SILENCE* can be DANGEROUS in a time where *SILENCE* needs to be BROKEN and SPOKEN! When we CONDONE certain BEHAVIORS we now enable others to be JUSTIFIED in their BEHAVIOR! That BEHAVIOR then, becomes LETHAL because PRIDE will never allow us to SEE ourselves!

Then there are other times...

When you have to BREAK your SILENCE before you SUFFER in SILENCE!

Beloveds! We have to make sure we are ACCEPTING the TRUTH and not ASSUMING things are TRUE or ACCEPTING it as a TRUTH!

Beloveds! Some people want BENEFITS and ACCESS they haven't SACRIFICED or LABORED for! #Don'tBeUsed

Beloveds! Some people want PRIVILEGES with no RESPONSIBILITIES! #Don'tBeFooled

Remember! Some people ONLY want to know your NEXT MOVE so they can MOVE before you or make the SAME MOVE! #BeWise

Beloveds! Every VOICE that sounds GENUINE is not a "GENUINE VOICE of CONCERN" but could actually be a "NOSEY VOICE of an OPPONENT" who's playing CHESS with you and wants to make a MOVE on you! #StayWoke

Beloveds! It is vital to know *"WHO WE ARE,"* then we won't have the desire to be IMPRESSIVE to others in hopes of being ACCEPTED by them! Sometimes we don't realize we're still on a QUEST to IMPRESS and a SEARCH for SIGNIFICANCE!

Don't allow the FEAR of the *UNKNOWN* make you stay in something *KNOWN* just because you are AFRAID of what you *DON'T KNOW!*

We can't tell anyone that we've BEEN THROUGH what we never CAME THROUGH! It's time to actually *COME THROUGH* what we're GOING THROUGH because somebody is waiting on us to get them THROUGH!

Remember "LOOK LIKE and SEEM LIKE" don't always make it REAL! Just because it *LOOKS LIKE IT or SEEMS LIKE IT* doesn't necessarily mean that's what IT'S LIKE!

Sometimes people act like they just don't UNDERSTAND but in all actuality they do UNDERSTAND! It's the UNDERSTANDING they don't want to *UNDER-STAND* because they don't like what IT means! They don't want to STAND UNDER the MEANING! Sometimes, you just have tell people "Oh you UNDERSTAND! You just DON'T want to STAND UNDER what IT MEANS!"

When we come to the END of ourselves; a place of LIMITS and a place where our abilities END then *GOD* steps in with NO LIMITS which is a place where HE never ENDS! See, when we MOVE out of *GOD's* way we MOVE *"LIMITS"* out of our WAY and then we MOVE into a *"LIMITLESS"* place! A place where there are NO LIMITS!

Frequently we have to *STOP* to do a *"RELATIONSHIP CHECK"* to make sure we haven't slipped into RELIGION while doing RELIGIOUS things! If gone UNCHECKED we can become RELIGIOUS without RELATIONSHIP and FELLOWSHIP!

SHAKE YOURSELF! This is *OUT* of your CONTROL so you can't let it CONTROL you!

Don't allow your DISSATISFACTION to disturb your SATISFACTION!

You can't WATCH GOD and WATCH IT! Just WATCH GOD DO IT!

We can't blame it on DISTRACTIONS when we allowed the DISTRACTIONS!

Whenever we CHOOSE what GOD DOESN'T want it's already doomed because GOD DIDN'T want IT!

EFFECTIVE LIVING produces an EFFECTIVE WITNESSS!

Sometimes we need to JUST WAIT!

You have to FINISH THIS before you START THAT!

IDENTITY- is *WHO* you are!

CHARACTER- is *WHAT* you do!

REPUTATION- is *HOW* people view you!

CHARACTER is not the same as REPUTATION, although REPUTATION is an estimation of HOW others see you based off of HOW you do WHAT you do! Just because it's HOW they view YOU doesn't mean it's WHO YOU ARE but if not careful WHAT YOU continuously *DO* will tell WHO YOU ARE! Remember, CHARACTER is what *TELLS* not what's *TOLD!* REPUTATION is what's TOLD! CHARACTER is what's SEEN therefore it *TELLS!* REPUTATION is what's SAID therefore it was *TOLD!* "WHO ARE YOU"

In others words...

Your *REPUTATION* and your *CHARACTER* should match your *IDENTITY!* What they "SEE" and what they "SAY" should match WHO YOU ARE!

Don't TAKE ON unnecessary BURDENS and now FALSE BURDENS are TAKING you OUT!

Don't MISTAKE folk who show up as SUPPORTERS, some people are showing up because they're NOSEY!

STOP running down behind folk trying to be FRIENDS with them! *"REAL FRIENDS"* don't send you on a *"WILD GOOSE CHASE"* just to be their FRIEND! Sometimes you just have to be FRIENDS with the FOLK who's trying to be FRIENDS with you!

It's TIME to VALUE YOU!

We have to *STOP TOLERATING* GOD until we get our *DESIRES* and actually *LIKE BEING* with GOD while we're waiting on our *DESIRES!* Honestly, we'll get our DESIRES sooner when GOD becomes our *DESIRE!*

There are some things that *WILL* happen INTENTIONALLY with the *INTENT* to *BLESS* you! Take the *BLESSING* and be *BLESSED!* Don't talk yourself out of it when it happens! EMBRACE IT! Besides, it's supposed to happen ONE DAY! ONE DAY is supposed to happen SOMEDAY and SOMEDAY can happen ANY DAY and ANY DAY can be your DAY!

We *ALL* have an OPPORTUNITY to learn the same thing BUT we don't *ALL* take ADVANTAGE of APPLYING the same things we've learned! Don't miss the chance to USE what you KNOW!

If we KNOW everything how can we LEARN anything! If we KNOW everything we can't be TAUGHT nothing! #BeHumble

Beloveds! WRONG LOVE will never be RIGHT! WRONG LOVE will never LOVE you RIGHT! LOVE can't LOVE RIGHT when it's WRONG! LOVING you WRONG will never be RIGHT!

Stop LOVING the WRONG one and LOVE the one who's RIGHT!

When you LOVE the WRONG person that's possibly *"WHY"* that person can never seem to LOVE you RIGHT because their LOVE will never be ENOUGH and you'll never be SATISFIED with their LOVE!

Beloveds! Not *ONLY* do we need to HEAR what GOD is SAYING but we also need to SEE what He's SAYING!

We wouldn't have to wear MASKS when *OUTSIDE* with others if we dealt with us *(while)* on the *INSIDE*!

Once we are CONSISTENT there will be CHANGE! CHANGE doesn't know what to CHANGE into because we are CONSISTENTLY INCONSISTENT bringing INCONSISTENCIES to our CHANGE!

DO NOT let the enemy *TRICK* you out of your PROCESS trying to get to PROGRESS!

You are going to need the PROCESS *"The Steps"* by which the PROGRESS is produced in order to help you SUSTAIN and MAINTAIN in the place you're going to! DON'T ALLOW the enemy to make you feel like there is nothing over HERE all because you want to get over THERE! Listen, the enemy doesn't mind you *"Getting There"* he just doesn't want you to *"Stay There"*! He knows if you can't APPRECIATE your HERE you'll ABUSE your THERE!

DON'T allow the enemy to *ROB* you of all the greatness of HERE because he knows it's the very thing that's going to keep you THERE! If you *MISS* those vital, essential and valuable things which are also the most important things while you're HERE you won't be able to stay THERE! Oftentimes the very thing that we're dissatisfied with HERE is actually the thing designed to take us THERE! Don't abuse your HERE for a place called THERE!

Beloveds! When people start MEANING what they SAY and SAYING what they MEAN that's when they'll start DOING what they SAID opposed to DOING what they MEANT to SAY!

Some of you are CONSTANTLY getting FRUSTRATED with people that are simply DOING what they MEAN and not what they SAY!

Some people DON'T MEAN what they're SAYING, that's why they CAN'T DO what they SAID! *It's just that simple...*

Sometimes you're witnessing people DO what they MEANT to SAY instead of DOING what they SAID! What they MEANT to SAY is what they actually MEAN and that's why they're DOING exactly what they DIDN'T SAY! Their ACTIONS are SAYING what they DIDN'T SAY!

STOP getting UPSET with people who DON'T DO what they SAY and start paying more ATTENTION to what they DIDN'T SAY which presents itself through their *"ACTIONS and DEEDS"!* These are patterns set up in their lives to show you they DON'T "MEAN" what they SAY; therefore they CAN'T DO what they SAID!

STOP getting MAD with folk because you *WON'T* accept what they're SHOWING you!

DON'T get ANGRY with people because their *ACTIONS* are speaking LOUD and CLEAR simply because it's not what you want to *HEAR!* They DON'T MEAN what they SAY beloved! They MEAN what they DO!

Remember, <u>it's hard to DO what you DON'T MEAN without it eventually showing that you DON'T MEAN IT! PAY ATTENTION! People are SHOWING you what they MEAN; you just have to BELIEVE it!</u>

Sometimes we are still dealing with the *STING* of the *PAST* and RESPONDING and REACTING *INAPPROPRIATELY* to things *NOW* because of what happened *THEN!* At times we're RESPONDING and REACTING *IMPROPERLY* to *PRESENT* situations because of the experiences of the *PAST!* Sometimes our RESPONSE is a REACTION to an OLD HURT which is affecting our ability to be HEALED NOW! It's just not fair to our *FUTURE* to continue to REACT and RESPOND in a NEW place with an OLD wound! We have to be HEALED from the *PAST* in order to give our *PRESENT* a *FUTURE!*

STOP getting MAD with FOLK who WON'T RESPECT the *GOD in YOU* when they DON'T RESPECT the *GOD of YOU!* How are they going to RESPECT *YOU* when they DON'T RESPECT *GOD!*

It's HARD to get people to UNDERSTAND a spiritual *YOU* when they can't UNDERSTAND a spiritual *GOD!* So, STOP getting MAD with folk who DON'T UNDERSTAND *YOU* when they DON'T UNDERSTAND *GOD!*

Continue to be faithful in SOWING SEEDS and GOD will continue to be faithful in MULTIPLYING and INCREASING your SEED!

There's a difference in *GIVING GOD our BEST* and *GIVING GOD what's LEFT!*

If you DON'T ENDURE the *HARDSHIP* to get to your PROMISE you'll return to the *SHIP* that has PASSED, then you might MESS around and MISS IT all the WAY around when all you had to do was *HOLD ON* because GOD was on the WAY! *"HE who is COMING will COME and HE will not TARRY "* but YOU have to ENDURE while HE'S COMING and until HE COMES! He's COMING but where will you be when He COMES?

DON'T be DISTRACTED by somebody *"COMING INTO"* a BLESSING and you are *"ALREADY IN"* a BLESSING!

Beloved! You WASTE TIME when you DON'T MAKE UP your MIND! DON'T WASTE valuable TIME simply because you won't MAKE UP your MIND! It's TIME for you to MAKE your MIND UP!

Sometimes, you have to GO through to GET through to COME through to COME to!

The MORE TIME you *WASTE* paying attention to somebody else in the race, is the MORE TIME you *LOSE* in the race! The MORE TIME you're *WASTING* is the MORE TIME you're *LOSING!* Wasting Time is Losing Time!

SIT DOWN and let GOD STAND UP!

STEP BACK and let GOD STEP FORWARD!

NO! It's NOT EASY when you *LET GO* but it's NOT HARD when you *LET GOD!*

The *VERY THING* you won't *LET GO* is the *SAME THING* you won't *LET GOD!* As long as you're HOLDING IT, GOD can't HOLD IT! As long as you're HOLDING ON to IT, GOD doesn't have to HOLD ON to IT! LET GO and LET GOD!

Your STORM might *WAKE* you OUT of your SLEEP but DON'T let it *TAKE* you OUT of your PEACE!

DON'T allow the THING designed to get you IN FOCUS to get you OUT of FOCUS! The *VERY THING* that's trying to get you OFF FOCUS could be the *VERY THING* used to get you to FOCUS IN! Sometimes you DON'T PAY ATTENTION to IT until you PAY ATTENTION to IT!

Listen! Sometimes GOD will use "YOUR TRIAL" just to get you to where He *WANTS* you to be in order to get you where you *NEED* to be!

Don't let the enemy's NOTHING mess with your SOMETHING! Don't *MAJOR* in *MINOR* things! Remember it's NOTHING MAJOR it's just a MINOR NOTHING!

Observation is a WISE TOOL! You don't ALWAYS have to SAY ANYTHING but you need to WATCH EVERYTHING!

There's a difference in GOING THROUGH and knowing *HOW* to GO THROUGH what you're GOING THROUGH! One of its most vital aspects is just that *"GOING THROUGH"!* It's also *HOW* you get your TESTIMONY! You went THROUGH your TEST, PAST IT and received your MONY: *a status, role or function or a personal quality or kind of behavior that was only produced by your* TEST!

Your EXPERIMENT comes to an *END* so your EXPERIENCE can *BEGIN!* Your TEST was just an EXPERIMENT designed to give you EXPERIENCE! Now it's time to use what you *GAINED* through your *TEST!* The duration of a TEST comes with an EXPIRATION date!

The best way to GET HIGH is to GET LOW! The *LOWER* you *GO* the *HIGHER* you *GO!* You want to GET HIGH you betta GET LOW! The more HUMBLED you are the HIGHER the ELEVATION! So how LOW can you GO?

The best way to GO UP is to GO DOWN! DON'T mistake what seems to be GOING DOWN as if it's not GOING back UP! What *GOES UP* must *COME DOWN* but I submit, when you're in GOD if it *GOES DOWN* it's got to *COME* back *UP!*

Be careful because when you *GIVE* up *SOMETHING* you might have to *GIVE* over to *SOMETHING!*

Don't *ALLOW* your CONDITION to REPOSITION you *OUT* of the WILL of GOD! DON'T let your CONDITION POSITION you AHEAD of GOD and cause you to get there BEFORE GOD, and now you still have to *WAIT* on GOD! DON'T jump out BEFORE HIM and PREMATURELY move in FRONT of HIM!

Don't *ALLOW* the enemy to make you *STEP OUT* of the timeline of GOD and all the time your BLESSING was coming at the APPOINTED TIME! Beloved, don't *STEP OUT* of TIME! GOD is on the way at the APPOINTED TIME!

Do *NOT* become too FASCINATED with an IDEA and never step into the REALITY of it! *DON'T* just become the IDEAL THING but never become the ACTUAL THING!

Some BREAKTHROUGHS are tied to some SACRIFICES!

The MORE SACRIFICE we *GIVE*, the MORE BREAKTHROUGHS we *RECEIVE!* DON'T allow a LACK of SACRIFICE to cause a LACK of SUPERNATURAL FAVOR! Your NEXT SACRIFICE could be your NEXT PRAISE!

Your NEXT GIVING to GOD could be your NEXT GETTING from GOD! We have GIVE to GOD to GET from GOD!

Don't WASTE your PRAISE on IT but PRAISE on IT!

DON'T you MOVE when you're CONFUSED!

Don't let a MINOR NOTHING become a MAJOR SOMETHING!

Don't allow the enemy to *FRUSTRATE* where YOU ARE because of where YOU'RE NOT!

The DOOR might be *OPENED* but you need to know *HOW* to WALK THROUGH the DOOR and *WHAT* to *DO* when you get in the DOOR!

Don't let your natural ability to SEE become your *SIN* but let your spiritual SEEING become your *FAITH* to BELIEVE!

GOD wants US to deal with OUR THOUGHTS before the THOUGHT becomes a WORD and that WORD becomes an ACTION and the ACTION becomes a HABIT and the HABIT becomes OUR CHARACTER and now THAT CHARACTER becomes US!

The enemy *WORKS* in HIDDEN PLACES and his first *TACTIC* is ISOLATION! If he can HIDE you then he can *WORK* on you!

STOP wasting TIME dealing with things that DON'T MATTER!

If folk DON'T want to accept WHO you are, let them stay WHERE they are! If they DON'T want to recognize the WHO in the WHAT, leave them right WHERE they are! If they DON'T want to acknowledge WHO and WHAT you are, let them remain WHERE you're NOT! Your fight for ACCEPTANCE *"WHO"*, RECOGNITION *"WHAT"*, and POSITION *"WHERE"* is OVER! You know *WHO YOU ARE!*

We have LESS struggles the MORE we SUBMIT to GOD! The MORE we SUBMIT the MORE POWER we get! The MORE we SUBMIT the MORE we can RESIST!

If the *SPIRIT MAN* is not in TACT the *REST* of *MAN* will be out of WACK!

The enemy DON'T mind you DOING STUFF, he just DON'T want you to KNOW WHAT you're DOING! He's NOT threatened by WHAT you're DOING he's threatened by you KNOWING WHAT you're DOING!

Beloveds! An UNATTENDED *DEVICE* from the ENEMY will later become an UNINTENTIONAL *PITFALL* for YOU! #PayAttention

GOD wants to PROCESS us to PROGRESS but the ENEMY wants us to PROGRESS without PROCESS! He doesn't mind us GETTING IT because he knows the SECRET! We're *NOT GONNA KEEP IT* if we haven't mastered *TITHING, SOWING, GIVING,* being a *GOOD STEWART,* a *BLESSING* and *INVESTING!* We'll be able to GET IT but we won't be able to KEEP IT!

Don't ABANDON your FEELINGS! Oftentimes it's *NOT* your FEELINGS it's the EXPRESSION of your FEELINGS! It's the AFFECT that your FEELINGS have on you that's causing an EFFECT to the person that you're EXPRESSING them to! Just work on *"WHEN* and *HOW"* to EXPRESS *"WHAT"* you are FEELING! Don't ABANDON your FEELINGS for the sake of someone else's FEELINGS! Your FEELINGS are just as IMPORTANT too! You just need WISDOM on *"WHEN* and *HOW"* to SHARE your FEELINGS! Whatever you do, please DON'T ABANDON your FEELINGS because you DON'T know *HOW* to DELIVER what you're FEELING! Just work on *HOW* to DELIVER *"WHAT"* you FEEL! It's *NOT* always *HOW* you FEEL, sometimes it's *HOW* you DELIVER *WHAT* you FEEL!

The last bit of *WISDOM* I have for you regarding your *FEELINGS* is don't ABANDON them APPROACH them and then APPROPRIATE them!

Something Else To Ponder…

IF GOD *DIDN'T SAY IT…*

DON'T YOU *DO IT…*

IF GOD *SAID IT…*

THEN *DO IT…*

AS I PONDER

3 INSPIRATIONS

Job 32:8 | KJV

"But [there is] a spirit in man: and the inspiration of the Almighty giveth them understanding."

Your GREATEST QUALITY and COMMODITY is BEING YOU!

Your DREAMS are just a DREAM until you make them LIVE!

Choose to be a LIFE CHANGER! In LIFE you will either CHANGE IT or be CHANGED by IT!

GET UP from there and *STOP* focusing on what DIDN'T WORK and ask GOD to show you what WILL WORK!

STOP wasting TIME and ENERGY crying over what DOESN'T WORK and DO something that DOES WORK!

Sometimes you have to DECREE and DECLARE that I have the spirit of *"THE UNTOUCHABLES"!* The enemy may try to "TOUCH" areas of your life or even things in your life but you must REFUSE to be *"TOUCHED"* by the *TOUCH!* You have to refuse to be AFFECTED, thus making you *"UNTOUCHABLE"!* The mere fact that you have decided to be "UNAFFECTED" makes the enemy's plan "INEFFECTIVE"!

Beloved! You can be in such a place in your SPIRITUAL LIFE with GOD that when TEMPTATIONS come to TEMPT you, you won't even be TEMPTED by the TEMPTATION that came to TEMPT you!

Simply Put...

The TEMPTATION that used to TEMPT you won't be a TEMPTATION for you!

Speak a CREATIVE WORD that will produce a CREATIVE MIRACLE!

Sometimes you have to DECREE and DECLARE that *"I'M A CHANGE AGENT"!*

FAITH doesn't LEAVE us sometimes we LEAVE the FAITH! FAITH doesn't WAIVER although at times we WAIVER in our FAITH! FAITH is CONSTANT and its PRESENT even when we find ourselves CONSTANTLY INCONSISTENT in our FAITH we can still grab a hold to NOW FAITH which is FAITH NOW!

Let your FAITH *INITIATE* your MIRACLE!

We are the proof of OUR PRAYERS! We don't have to TELL each other HOW MUCH or HOW MANY times we PRAY, we should SEE PRAYER as YOU because it becomes YOU! It's a LIFESTYLE; it becomes your *"STYLE of LIFE"!* PRAYER is YOU and YOU become the fruit of your PRAYERS! Now BE the PRAYERS that YOU PRAY! Don't TURN a SPIRITUAL EXPERIENCE into a RELIGIOUS ACT full of RITUALS! Although PRAYER is RELIGIOUS *(a spirit of reverence toward God; applying to whatever pertains to faith or worship; to be Faithful or devout)* and it can be considered a RITUAL *(a system or collection of religious or other rites, any practice or pattern of behavior regularly performed in a set manner)* but DON'T become RELIGIOUS *(Pious implies constant attention to, and extreme conformity with, outward observances with your)* RITUAL! AMEN...

Let's Pray...

LORD not only do we WANT your PRESENCE but we WANT your GLORY! LORD not only do we WANT a VISITATION from you but we NEED a HABITATION from you in *JESUS NAME* we *pray!*

When we STRETCH our FAITH we OPEN the GATE for MIRACLES!

Listen, if you *PRAISE GOD* in "NOT ENOUGH" He'll bring you out with MORE than ENOUGH! When we *BLESS HIM* with what's "NOT ENOUGH" He will *BLESS US* with "MORE than ENOUGH"! However, if we try to *HOLD ON* to what's already not ENOUGH it doesn't make room for "MORE than ENOUGH"! We have to allow room for *GOD* to *STRETCH* our *NOT ENOUGH* into *MORE* than *ENOUGH!*

The *Spirit* of the *LORD* is waiting for a *WORD* to be released to activate but you need to OPEN your MOUTH and SAY!

Sometimes you just have to OPEN your MOUTH and say *"I AM* the *ACTUALITY* of *GOD'S REALITY! I'M* not a *FIGMENT* of *GOD'S IMAGINATION! I AM* the *IMAGE* for the *NATION"!*

Sometimes you just have to have a PRAISE BREAK! You have to keep PRAISING and watch the *BREAKING!* As you PRAISE it *BREAKS!* Keep PRAISING and watch *IT* keeps *BREAKING!* You got to keep *PRAISING* and watch the *BREAKING!* Remember *PRAISE - BREAKS!*

Beloved! GOD wants to send YOU IN to bring CHANGE and not to be CHANGED!

Don't allow LOW EXPECTATIONS to bring *DOWN* your EXPECTATIONS for ELEVATION! We have to *EXPECT GOD* to do the *UNEXPECTED* and *EXPECT HIM* to do the *EXPECTED!*

When you make *"The MOVE"* FEAR then has to *MOVE!* When you take *"The STEP"* FEAR then has to *STEP!* Remember FEAR only works when you are FEARFUL but once you finally decide to make *The MOVE,* you move into LESS FEAR and the more you *MOVE* into LESS FEAR is the more you *MOVE* in LESS FEAR! As you keep moving in LESS FEAR is the more you *MOVE* without FEAR and into a FEARLESS place! STOP allowing FEAR to take you into a FEARFUL place and START taking FEAR with you to a FEARLESS place! You may be experiencing or have experienced some FEARS but DON'T allow FEAR to STOP you from making *The MOVE* when you know it's GOD take FEAR with you while you are making *The MOVE!*

Remember FEAR *"ONLY"* works when you are FEARFUL!

Beloveds! We have to EXPECT the UNEXPECTED! THINK the UNTHINKABLE and IMAGINE the UNIMAGINABLE!

You can't believe GOD and DON 'T BELIEVE GOD!

ASK AGAIN but this time ASK with GOD in MIND and ASK with the *MIND of CHRIST!*

GOD *LOVES* you! Now you have to *LOVE* you! It's the best way to show others HOW to LOVE you! When you LOVE yourself it sets a standard on HOW you are to be LOVED!

When you know that God *LOVES* you and you *LOVE* yourself, it changes the way you LOVE and the way you are LOVED! When you LOVE you RIGHT folk have NO other CHOICE but to LOVE you RIGHT! You set the tone for LOVE to be RIGHT in your LIFE just by LOVING yourself RIGHT!

You have a VOICE that could make ALL the DIFFERENCE! Your VOICE could be the VOICE needed to CHANGE the SOUND that somebody's been HEARING! Just think about what you could you SAY to them that could make ALL the DIFFERENCE in their LIFE! It could literally CHANGE the WAY they HEAR and the WAY they've been HEARING all their LIVES!

Your *NEXT ELEVATION* might be locked up in your ELIMINATION! When you're ready to take the *ELEVATOR to ELEVATION* then you may have to be the ELIMINATOR to some folk that need to be ELIMINATED before you're *ELEVATED!*

Your *NEXT INCREASE* might be locked up in your DECREASE! When you're ready to experience *GREATER GROWTH* in your LIFE you also have to be ready to cut down the SIZE of folk in your LIFE and the NUMBER of people circling your LIFE!

Your *NEXT PROMOTION* could be locked up in your NEXT PRAISE! You might have to *CHANGE* your *ROW* because some folk NEXT to you can't GO! Besides, you're gonna need MORE room for this PRAISE! Now, can you imagine the SIZE of the PROMOTION!

Your ability to be PATIENT is your ability to tolerate DELAY without COMPLAINT! It's the very thing that's PERFECTING meaning MATURING you! Always remember, the thing you're WAITING ON is not the thing that COMPLETES you but rather your ability to WAIT for IT is COMPLETING you!

STAND UP in *WHO YOU ARE,* so *WHO YOU ARE* can STAND OUT!

Don't be afraid to be called PECULIAR! GOD called you that! PECULIAR people can do some STRANGE and UNCOMMON things! PECULIAR doesn't *ONLY* mean STRANGE but it also means SPECIAL! When you do something STRANGE with your SPECIAL self, you're also doing something SPECIAL!

You have to be WILLING to do the UNCOMMON and what's not POPULAR in this HOUR to effect CHANGE!

Something Else To Reflect On...

Your ABILITY to WAIT for the THING you're WAITING for is what makes you PERFECT *(mature)* and LACKING nothing! NOT when you finally get what you're WAITING for but while you're WAITING for IT!

MY REFLECTIONS

4 ILLUMINATION

Daniel 5:14 | NAS

"Now I have heard about you that a spirit of the gods is in you, and that illumination, insight and extraordinary wisdom have been found in you."

Not only is GOD a JUST GOD but HE is JUST GOD!

The enemy will try to change your POSITION because of your current CONDITION!

Sometimes GOD will allow you to *GO THROUGH* to see WHO'S with you.

GOD supplies NEEDS but HE grants WANTS! You DON'T have to be there for GOD to SUPPLY your NEEDS but you do NEED to be there to GET what you WANT! The SUPPLY is just SUPPLIED; the NEED is just MET but you NEED to be a RECIPIENT to GET what you WANT!

SUPRESSION is not HEALING nor is it DELIVERANCE!

FORGETTING about IT doesn't mean we're HEALED or DELIVERED from IT!

Just because we haven't been AROUND IT, doesn't mean we're DELIVERED from it!

Just because IT'S HIDING doesn't mean IT'S NOT THERE!

ISOLATION is not DELIVERANCE

We are not being DELIVERED until it HURTS! We're not HEALED or DELIVERED from IT if we CAN'T REVISIT IT and not be AFFECTED by IT!

You can't make an *ALLIANCE* with your FLESH! Your FLESH will *TELL ON* you every *OPPORTUNITY* it gets!

Our own FLESH will TELL US and TELL OTHERS what we're not DELIVERED from!

If nothing else is HAPPENING in the place you're currently in, then there's a possibility you've *MAXED OUT* all that place can give! You now have to MOVE ON to the place where it's HAPPENING!

You can't expect to get something NEW out of something OLD! Sometimes it's TIME to MOVE!

Sometimes in decision making we have to STOP and ASK some questions! *"IF I DO that NOW, then what am I going to DO LATER and WHAT affect is IT going to have on me LATER"?* Always remember if there's a NOW then there's a LATER! Don't allow the DECISION you make NOW to mess you up LATER!

When considering people, places or things you have to STOP and ASK the question *"Is this going to HELP me or HINDER me"?*

Not ONLY is GOD EVERYTHING! HE has to be everything to YOU! Although HE is everything, HE also has to be YOUR everything!

When you SHIFT into the NEW, GOD will SHIFT things to ACCOMODATE you!

Beloved! You WON'T make it over THERE until you're CONTENT over HERE! Don't *MISS or OVERLOOK* what's HERE for always LOOKING over THERE! If not careful, your place called "THERE" can make you DISCONTENT with your place HERE which is PURPOSED to take you THERE!

Some things are DESIGNED to PROVOKE you into your DESTINY!

Beloveds! There's NOTHING ELSE to LEARN if we already know EVERYTHING! PRIDE will never ALLOW us to know PAST what we THINK we *(already)* know!

We can be MISPLACED and DISPLACED while in the RIGHT PLACE!

Beloveds! We can be IN GOD but still going IN the wrong direction IN GOD!

The enemy doesn't have to *USE* us when we're already *USING* ourselves! Sometimes we OPEN the DOOR for the DOOR OPENER *"Baal Peor"* The Lord of the *OPENING of TRICKS"!* He doesn't have to TRICK us when we're already TRICKING ourselves because we don't know how to CLOSE OUR OWN DOOR! SHUT the DOOR! CLOSE the DOOR to your OWN HOUSE!

Beloveds, to some people you are the BEST THING since *"SLICED BREAD"* until you start *SLICING* into their *BREAD!* When you start *CUTTING* into those THINGS they've been operating in now the WAR begins!

Beloveds! When folk can no longer GLEAN or RECEIVE from you, it's because they THINK they KNOW MORE than you! In some cases that could very well be TRUE as it relates to the area of KNOWLEDGE; however remaining *TEACHABLE* will afford us the opportunity to RECEIVE what we don't KNOW by way of REVELATION KNOWLEDGE! KNOWLEDGE and REVELATION KNOWLEDGE are not the same!

Beloveds! When folk feel they have become your EQUAL they now enter into a *"POWER STRUGGLE"* with you which is not a STRUGGLE for you because you don't FIGHT for what's already ON you nor do you have to PROVE what's already PROVEN! YOU ARE the PROOF of what's IN you!

Just because you can't SEE your WAY doesn't mean there's NO WAY! Sometimes SEEING our WAY can block us from SEEING the WAY simply because it's NOT our WAY!

There's a difference in *"STARTING OVER"* and a *"FRESH START"!*

The enemy will pervert the NATURAL FEAR God gives us to be aware of DANGER and will turn it into a SPIRIT of FEAR that GRIPS us because we are AFRAID!

Your AGITATION will bring FORTH your EXPECTATION!

Isn't it AMAZING how we CAN spend time WAITING for "GOOD ENOUGH" to turn "GOOD" but we CAN'T WAIT for "GOOD"!

People who *"WAIT"* get DESTINY and those who *"CAN'T WAIT"* get DESPERATE!

Some people are PURPOSE SEEKERS while others are PURPOSE DRIVEN! PURPOSE SEEKERS start a lot of things they don't finish! PURPOSE DRIVEN not only start but they finish! PURPOSE SEEKERS will always envy PURPOSE DRIVEN people! Simply because you are not trying to *FIND IT*, you already *FOUND IT!* You're not trying to discover *"WHO YOU ARE"* you know *"WHO YOU ARE"!* At some point in LIFE we were ALL PURPOSE SEEKERS however some *FOUND* the PURPOSE they were *SEEKING* and they became *DRIVEN* by that PURPOSE while others are still *SEEKING* to *FIND IT!*

People will become JEALOUS of you NOT because you've MADE the MOVE but because YOU ARE the MOVE! A MOVE is nothing without you knowing WHO YOU ARE!

Trying to figure out whether it's GOD or YOU? Your *"EMOTIONS"* and your *"FEELINGS"* will let you know when it's YOU! When they are in OPERATION and are the INSPIRATION it's a great INDICATOR it's YOU!

Sometimes you're NOT being HELD BACK from DOING IT; you're being HELD BACK by NOT DOING IT!

That which you MEDITATE *(picture, reflect and ponder)* on and allow to PENETRATE *(pierce and affect deeply)* thus causing it to PERMEATE *(spread and run through)* it will then begin to SATURATE *(drench and impregnate to the fullest)* now it's gonna start to MARINATE *(soak through)* and at the END of the DAY it's gonna put a COMMAND and a DEMAND on you to DEMONSTRATE *(display openly, exhibit, show, manifest and testify)* what you ATE! What's IN YOU got to come OUT of YOU!

It's not GOD HOLDING OUT on us, most of the time it's GOD WAITING on us! GOD is WAITING on us to GET READY for what HE'S been READY to do! GOD GOT IT! HE'S just waiting on us to GET IT!

The LORD wants to be USED by YOU that's why HE'S UPON YOU!

Sometimes GOD has to allow some things to GRAZE you to GROW you!

Sometimes GOD has to BREAK you to MAKE you!

Sometimes GOD has to allow PRESSURE in your life to produce POWER out of your life!

Sometimes GOD has to let you GO through PAIN to PULL the POWER out of the PAIN!

Sometimes GOD has to take you to a PLACE of *"WHAT NOT"* to show you *"WHAT NOT"* to do in the next PLACE!

Sometimes GOD has to allow *"SOME THINGS"* to take place in LIFE to show you *"WHAT THINGS"* are NOT allowed in LIFE!

Sometimes GOD has to let folk WALK OUT of your LIFE just to show you THEY never should've have WALKED INTO your LIFE!

Sometimes GOD has to allow you to be AFFECTED just to see the EFFECT in order to see if you'll PASS the TEST!

Sometimes GOD has to allow a situation to GET a RESPONSE from you just to see what kind of REACTION comes OUT of you! Your RESPONSE and your REACTION means EVERYTHING and can often determine ALOT of THINGS!

Sometimes GOD has to let you LOSE IT in order to GAIN IT!

Sometimes GOD has to allow situations to MAKE you SCREAM in the NATURAL in order to OPEN up a STREAM of blessings to FLOW in the SUPERNATURAL!

Sometimes GOD will let you FALL so you'll experience the POWER of getting BACK UP!

Sometimes GOD will let you experience being DOWN and OUT so that you'll APPRECIATE what it means to be UP and OUT!

Sometimes your JOY is locked up in your TRUTH!

We don't have a problem SAYING we have a problem DOING! Our problem IS not *SAYING* our problem *IS DOING!* It's hard to demonstrate what you SAY if you don't MEAN what you're SAYING! Every time we SAY what we don't MEAN and don't INTEND to DO it's now considered a LIE!

The reason why we still have so many TEMPTATIONS is because SECRETLY we still WANT them!

A VICTIM can never *SEE* when they're VICTIMIZING others; they only *SEE* when they're being VICTIMIZED by others!

When SATAN is in OPERATION you'll also find ACCUSATION!

Oftentimes your TEST, TRIAL and STORM brings *WEAKNESS* to you in order to bring STRENGTH out of you!

Sometimes it's not *UNTIL* your TEST, TRIAL and STORM that you FIND OUT what you've been CALLED to do!

You may have *BEAT* your enemy "THAT TIME" and trying to figure out *WHY* you're struggling to *BEAT* him "THIS TIME"! Might I suggest, you have to *INQUIRE* of *The* LORD "EVERYTIME"! There just might be a different strategy "EACH TIME" because the enemy studied your strategy from the "LAST TIME"!

Sometimes the enemy will try to make you think you completely *MISSED GOD* and in all actuality you just got there *BEFORE GOD* but now you're realizing you still have to WAIT for GOD! So just WAIT! You were actually CLOSER before you moved!

Just because you DON'T SEE IT, DON'T mean GOD didn't RELEASE IT!

Your ANSWER is in your PEACE! Your HEALING is your ANSWERS!

GOD will DO just what HE SAID as WE OBEY what HE SAID!

PLAGIARISM is not REVELATION! There's a difference!

INSPIRATION is not REVELATION either! There's a difference!

PRIDE will NEVER allow YOU to see YOURSELF! So it certainly WON'T let you CORRECT yourself! HOW can we CORRECT what we CAN'T see or even think is THERE! HOW are we going to see WHAT needs to be CORRECTED nevertheless HOW to CORRECT it! Always remember *"FLESH and PRIDE"* work together to HIDE YOU!

The enemy CARES NOTHING about you PROGRESSING, he CARES about you PROCESSING while you're PROGRESSING! DON'T try to get to PROGRESS without PROCESS; you might NOT KEEP the PROGRESS! You are a *REAL THREAT* to the enemy when you PROCESS with PROGRESS!

Our DIRECTION in GOD is directly linked to our TRUST in GOD! When we TRUST GOD we now allow HIM to DIRECT our PATH!

What's IN your VIEW can sometimes *BLOCK* what GOD is trying to DO and what HE'S trying to bring INTO your VIEW!

Sometimes you have to MOVE FROM to MOVE TO! In order to MOVE TO you have to MOVE FROM!

You DON'T have to be PERFECT to be in the PERFECT WILL of GOD! You just need to be *AGREEABLE* with the PERFECT WILL of GOD! You DON'T have to be PERFECT you just need to *ACCEPT* GOD'S PERFECT WILL over your life! Your ACCEPTANCE and AGREEMENT will PERFECT *(mature)* YOU! Your ACCEPTANCE and your AGREEMENT will PROGRESS YOU and bring PERFECTION *(growth)* out of YOU!

Are you still trying to WORK what's NOT WORKING? Just because it seems like things are NOT WORKING where you are doesn't mean GOD is NOT WORKING! HE'S just NOT WORKING there but HE IS WORKING somewhere! Sometimes you have to make the *MOVE* to where GOD is *MOVING* because that's where HE'S WORKING!

If there's NO MORE ROOM in a SPACE to *WORK* for you then GOD will MOVE you to a WORKING SPACE! A SPACE that'll *WORK* for you!

GOD is NOT looking for PERFECTION! He's already that! He's looking for PROGRESSION! YOU don't have to be PERFECT! GOD is already PERFECT and the PERFECT ONE is in YOU! Therefore PERFECTION is IN YOU but wants to come OUT of YOU! Your PROGRESSION brings forth GOD'S PERFECTION in you! Your PROGRESSION will manifest your PERFECTION *(maturity and growth)*! Just PROGRESS and let God PERFECT!

If something is HINDERING your PROGRESSION it will also HINDER your PERFECTION *(maturity and growth)*! If PROGRESSION is HINDERED than PERFECTION will also be HINDERED! We PERFECT *(become mature and grow)* because we PROGRESSED *(we advanced and moved forward)*!

If you GET RID of your HOPE, you GET RID of your VISION! If you GET RID of your VISION, you GET RID of your PROMISE! DON'T FORFEIT your PROMISE because you GAVE UP on your HOPE!

Another Thought To Ponder…

HOPE is in the FUTURE!

FAITH is right NOW!

HOPE *(hopes)* BELIEVES for it

but FAITH brings that BELIEF to NOW!

HOPE sets it up and FAITH brings it to pass!

THOUGHTS TO PONDER

5 INSIGHT

Proverbs 2:3 | AMP

"Yes, if you cry out for insight, and lift up your voice for understanding"

The *"KEYS"* to FINDING your PURPOSE is through REVELATION which only comes through RELATION which gives you INFORMATION about your DESTINATION! RELATIONSHIP with *The FATHER* transforms into REVELATION which transmits INFORMATION! However, we have to move from SALVATION to RELATION in order to receive this type of INFORMATION! Basically, it takes RELATION to know about our DESTINATION"!

You've been AFFECTED to be EFFECTIVE!

GOD had to use the FORMER you to produce RESULTS for the PRESENT you! Let your PAST work for you and NOT against you!

GOD doesn't want you to RELIVE the *STING* of the PAST but He wants you to RECOGNIZE why you were *STUNG!* You were *STUNG* to produce your OUTCOME! IT had to *STING* you to STIR you!

There's a difference in REMEMBERING and CONSIDERING! When you CONSIDER what you REMEMBER then you will DEMONSTRATE what you CONSIDERED!

There's a difference in RECALLING *"Remembering- Retrieving"* and RECOGNITION *"Recognizing – Identifying!"*

You can RECALL IT but you don't have to RECOGNIZE IT!

You can REMEMBER IT but you don't have to be AFFECTED by the MEMORY of IT!

A MENTAL ABSORPTION is *NOT* the same as a SPIRITUAL REVELATION!

Jesus had to give the people a NATURAL EXPLANATION of a SPIRITUAL REVELATION! Something they could UNDERSTAND in order to bring them UP to HIS UNDERSTANDING!

When you DISCOVER and UNCOVER what was COVERED you become a *THREAT* to the enemy!

WHEN your PERCEPTION changes in the SPIRITUAL realm, it places a demand on a POSITION change in the NATURAL realm!

Simply Put...

Your SPIRITUAL PERCEPTION changes your NATURAL PERSPECTIVE and your SPIRITUAL POSITION changes your NATURAL CONDITION!

If you ENTERTAIN IT you might become ENTERTAINING to IT!

Sometimes God will sit you down in a place called "WHAT NOT TO DO" just to show you "WHAT NOT TO DO" when it's time for you TO DO WHAT GOD has CALLED you TO DO!

DON'T MISS your ONE DAY by *LOOKING* for SOMEDAY!

Don't let COMPROMISE become your DEMISE!

Be careful because FEAR will make you FORGET that you got FAVOR!

Simply Put...

FEAR FORGETS FAVOR!

Remember, EXPECTATION pulls on REVELATION!

GUESS WHAT? It was the WARFARE UPON you that produced the GREATER GLORY in you!

A FAMINE will always tempt you to GO BACK but OBEDIENCE will BACK you OUT of a FAMINE!

Beloveds! Remember the ANOINTING is on the INSTRUCTIONS!

When CHRONOS *(natural time)* can't TELL TIME *(when SPRING TIME feels like FALL)* we're in the KAIROS (spiritual) TIME of GOD!

When DUE SEASON comes into SET TIME! When the TIME that was SET in HEAVEN *(Kairos)* comes down to meet up *"COLLIDE"* with the FULLNESS of TIME on the EARTH REALM*(Chronos)* you're in a SEASON of DUE! It's a SEASON were things are NOW DUE because things were PROCESSED in TIME and have FULFILLED the things within the TIMELINE of GOD on the EARTH; now it's TIME for things to be RELEASED to you because HEAVEN has already DECIDED that it's DUE to you in SET TIME *(in a TIME that was already SET)*!

Let Me Say It Like This...

When The FULLNESS of TIME is properly PROCESSED through TIME it will POSITION you for SET TIME because now its DUE SEASON for what was already DELIBERATED by the TIMELINE of GOD!

When we "WAIT ON" the LORD He'll keep us in OUR WAIT! When we "WAIT UPON" HIM, He gives us the STRENGTH to OUT WAIT the WAIT! When we WAIT in our OWN STRENGTH we don't have the ENDURANCE to WAIT until the end of the WAIT! When we WAIT in our OWN STRENGTH we don't have the LONGEVITY to WAIT OUT the WAIT! There's a difference *in "WAITING"* and *"WAITING UPON"* the LORD! Our WAITING is primarily done in our OWN STRENGTH but WAITING on the LORD is done with HIS STRENGTH!

DON'T let your NIGHT SEASON become a DARK SEASON! Just because it's NIGHT *(a time of obscurity)* doesn't mean it has to become DARK *(absence of light; wicked, evil)*!

Sometimes God will create a SITUATION to bring about a REALIZATION in order to bring forth a DIVINE REVELATION!

Beloved, there's a distinct difference between FORGIVENESS *(pardon, excuse, blot out, release, grace)* and REPENTANCE *(turning around, remorse, contrite, offering, sacrifice)*! FORGIVENESS doesn't mean we're TURNING AROUND and not RETURNING to IT; it just means we need to be EXCUSED and PARDONED from IT this TIME until we TURN AROUND to do IT again the next TIME!

Beloveds! Did you know that it's *NOT* always the MOVE sometimes it's the TIME! It maybe GOD'S WILL but it also needs to be HIS TIME!

Did you know that a PREMATURE MOVE doesn't ALWAYS mean we MISSED GOD, sometimes it just means we MOVED before GOD *(moved)* and now we have to WAIT for a MOVE of GOD! Don't MOVE now, just WAIT for GOD to MOVE!

Beloveds! Did you know that just because GOD PERMITS his WILL doesn't mean it's HIS PERFECT WILL at the TIME! There's a difference between PERMISSIBLE and PERFECT!

When there's A PROMISE over *YOUR LIFE*, you don't have to do TRICKS to get IT!

Your BREAKTHROUGH is contingent upon your FOLLOW THROUGH!

GREATER the SUFFERING GREATER the ANOINTING!

Your GREATEST area of STRUGGLE is your GREATEST area of SUCCESS! The GREATEST area of STRUGGLE can also be your GREATEST area of MINISTRY!

Sometimes you have to let people know "I'm not *WEAK* because I'm *MEEK!* I'm *MEEK* because of the *CHRIST* in *ME!*

Sometimes we have to *SIT BACK...RELAX...BREATH* in and *BREATH OUT!* THAT'S IT and THAT'S ALL! STOP IT! YOU'RE DOING TOO MUCH!

Whenever you find yourself in need of ANSWERS, always look for PEACE! When you find PEACE you will find GOD! The PEACE is where GOD is! Wherever the PEACE of GOD is, is where your ANSWER is! When YOU have PEACE from GOD, YOU will also have ANSWERS from GOD!

NO PEACE NO ANSWER!

NO PEACE NO GOD!

Beloveds! If they HATE you NOW, what are THEY GOING to DO LATER! Folk are NOT THREATENED by you NOW, it's WHAT your NOW have the POTENTIAL to DO LATER! It's YOUR NOW that tells THEM about YOUR LATER! They might be JEALOUS of you NOW but they're really THREATENED by you LATER!

Remember, people choose to BELIEVE what they want to BELIEVE knowing it's not the *CHARACTER* nor the *FRUIT* the person BEARS; however it JUSTIFIES their *BEHAVIOR* therefore bringing others down makes them look BETTER! If they can make you look like a MESS, it JUSTIFIES their MESS!

If everybody LIKE YOU you're *"NOT"* doing your JOB! When you start *"RUFFLING FEATHERS"* you know your JOB was done! The LIFE and MINISTRY of JESUS CHRIST made folk UNCOMFORTABLE! If everyone is COMFORTABLE around US, then WE need to CHECK our "LIVES and MINISTRY"!

The IMPRINT of your HANDPRINT should be at the BACK of the enemy's NECK!

We have to be "FLEXIBLE IN GOD" to be "AVAILABLE TO GOD"! Your *FLEXIBILITY* speaks of your *AVAILABILITY!*

STOP DOING TOO MUCH! It's STEALING your PEACE and ROBBING you of PEACE! It's the *UNNECESSARY* that brings *(on)* *UNNECESSARIES!*

Sometimes GOD will take you in the SAME DIRECTION but in a DIFFERENT WAY! Be *OPEN* to receive what GOD can do with the SAME THING but in DIFFERENT WAY!

Sometimes you want to DO IT, you just don't want the *RESPONSIBILITY* and *ACCOUNTABILITY* it takes to DO IT!

Sometimes GOD will use a DIFFERENT METHOD just to give us the SAME MESSAGE!

Sometimes what you NEED is already in your HAND! #LOOKAGAIN

Some are not "REAPING the BENEFITS" of where they've been *ASSIGNED* to simply because of *NOT* doing what they've been *ASSIGNED* to do! Fulfilling your ASSIGNMENT will get you the BENEFITS that are ATTACHED to what you've been *ASSIGNED* to do!

Things done AIMLESSLY with NO INTENT, PURPOSE or MEANING provides NO DIRECTION and only BEAT at the WIND with the INTENT of catching NOTHING! When things are done with PURPOSE we give it MEANING which gives it INTENT therefore you can REAP the BENEFITS that were INTENDED because you TOLD IT what to do and where to go! When things are done on PURPOSE you provide it with DIRECTION and INSTRUCTIONS!

Don't get accustomed to your CIRCUMSTANCE that now you sound like the CIRCUMSTANCE!

Beloved! You don't have to *SPEAK* the language of your CONDITION! RECONDITION your CONDITION to *SPEAK* your language! Make your CONDITION become CONDITIONED to another language!

NOT ONLY do we need TOOLS but we need to know *HOW to USE* those TOOLS! Listen, you don't have a problem DEFEATING the enemy; sometimes the problem is knowing *HOW to DEFEAT* him! YOU got IT but YOU got to USE IT! YOU got IT but YOU got to know HOW to USE IT! YOU have to APPLY what YOU know and YOU need to know HOW to USE what YOU got!

Sometimes a STRUGGLE with RESISTING the enemy is really a STRUGGLE with SUBMITTING to GOD! SUBMITTING to GOD makes RESISTING the enemy easy and then he will FLEE! He has to FLEE not just because we're RESISTING him but because he SEES our RESISTANTS is backed by our SUBMISSION! Our SUBMISSION to GOD gets us POWER from GOD!

PREMATURE MOVES don't always mean it wasn't *"A MOVE"* it just means you moved before *"THE MOVE"* was MATURE and COMPLETE! "The MOVE" wasn't completely READY it was still in PREPARATION! It was incomplete and you now have to *WAIT for GOD* to complete it!

PREMATURE MOVES doesn't necessarily mean you MISSED *"A MOVE of GOD"* either it could just mean you MOVED before *"The MOVE of GOD"* and you got there before GOD was MOVING and now you still have to WAIT for GOD to MOVE!

We aren't DRAWN AWAY by it; we're DRAWN AWAY by our lust for it!

Sometimes we say people *CHANGED* but in all *ACTUALITY* they just *BECAME* what was *IN* them!

Sometimes our STEPS will be made VERY CLEAR once we take STEPS to CLEAR our THINKING! Sometimes the way we're THINKING and the way we THINK is in the WAY of our CLARITY!

People who KNOW EVERYTHING just MISSED SOMETHING!

Some people CAN'T GO into your NEXT SEASON because some of them *DEVOURED* your LAST SEASON!

GOD knows we're NOT PERFECT but He expects our IMPERFECTIONS to have some PROGRESSION!

Something To Reflect On…

Some people want a "QUICK FIX" but they don't want "IT FIXED"! In order to "FIX IT" you have to be a willing participant in it being "FIXED"!

GOD DOESN'T DO

QUICK FIXES…

HE FIXES IT!

AS I REFLECT

6 ENCOURAGEMENT

2 Corinthians 1:4 | AMP

"Who comforts and encourages us in every trouble so that we will be able to comfort and encourage those who are in any kind of trouble, with the comfort with which we ourselves are comforted by God."

GOD is turning your CONDITIONAL PRAISE into an UNCONVENTIONAL PRAISE!

You're not just in a *SEASON of FAVOR*; you're in a *CLIMATE of FAVOR!* SEASON deals with SHORT- TERM but CLIMATE deals with LONG-TERM!

GOD is the SOURCE of the RESOURCE!

There's a *"RE"* over YOUR LIFE! And GOD is going DO IT AGAIN and AGAIN and AGAIN! He's going to make IT all ADD UP and MAKE SENSE to you ALL OVER AGAIN!

Instead of waking up with the FEAR of FAILING wake up with the FAITH of EXCELLING!

Instead of waking up with the FEAR of FALLING wake up with the FAITH knowing that GOD will KEEP you!

When ALL HELL *"BREAKS LOOSE"* it's an INDICATOR that BREAKTHROUGH is COMING THROUGH!

GOD is ALPHA and OMEGA the BEGINNING and the END! When He STARTS a thing He FINISHES it!

YOU don't have to try to *WIN* when JESUS has already *WON!* VICTORY belongs to YOU because IT was *WON* for YOU! Therefore you don't FIGHT for VICTORY you FIGHT from VICTORY!

When the enemy has a PLOT GOD has a PLAN!

When the enemy SHOWS UP it's an INDICATOR that you are GOING UP!

STOP ALLOWING the enemy to *DISCOMBOBULATE* you just because he *SABOTAGED* your first PLAN! Remember there's ALWAYS ANOTHER PLAN!

If you *PRAISED GOD for IT* you need to be there to *THANK GOD for IT!* Don't get WEARY and leave your place of PRAISE; you have to be there to receive the BLESSING that you PRAYED and PRAISED GOD for!

Sometimes you have to DECLARE to yourself that "*It's the NEW ME and the NOW ME and it looks GOOD ON ME*"!

ONE of the GREATEST POWERS you have is the POWER of BEING YOU! Can't NOBODY beat YOU at "*BEING YOU*" because there's ONLY ONE YOU! No one can BE a GREATER YOU than YOU!

Don't get STUCK in this week's *DEFEATS* and MISS next week's *VICTORIES!* Don't allow this week's *FAILURES* to MESS UP next week's *SUCCESSES!* GET OVER IT so you can GET ON with IT!

*YOU say... THEY say... HE says...SHE says...*BUT what did *GOD say*! Don't allow the OPINIONS of others or even yourself to make you forget WHAT GOD SAID!

The enemy can try to BLOCK YOU but he cannot STOP YOU! He can't STOP a person with an UNSTOPPABLE PRESS! A PRESS that CANNOT be STOPPED! Your PRESS is keeping you from STOPPING! Your PRESS is keeping you from being STOPPED! If you keep PRESSING you don't have to worry about being STOPPED!

When you're BUILT for IT, you DON'T BACK DOWN or QUIT!

You DON'T QUIT when you're BORN for IT!

Beloveds! GOD can take you from the land of "NOT ENOUGH" and cause you to surpass the land of "JUST ENOUGH" and then take you right into the land of "MORE THAN ENOUGH"! Trust Him Today and Be Encouraged!

Beloveds! STRENGTH without VULNERABILITY is nothing more than a STONE that cannot be MOVED! No matter how STRONG you are, you are STILL HUMAN and there will be some WEAKNESSES which only show you're HUMAN and not WEAK! *"It is in our WEAKNESSES that GOD'S STRENGTH is made PERFECT in us"*!

Your SILENT FRUSTRATION will ONE DAY be your LOUD VICTORY and SONG of PRAISE!

Sometimes you just have to SUFFER in SILENCE when GOD won't allow you to BREAK your SILENCE and all HE says to you is *"MY GRACES is SUFFICIENT for YOU"!* ONE DAY GOD will allow you to tell your STORY in DUE SEASON and it will be a TRUE TESTAMENT of GOD'S VICTORY in your LIFE! BE ENCOURAGED!

Remember, the TRUTH don't need NO HELP, it's already TRUE! A LIE has to FIGHT to prove it's TRUE which will never come TRUE!

Listen! When you ARE the TRUTH and you KNOW the TRUTH you don't have to chase down LIES in order to tell the TRUTH! You already KNOW the TRUTH; therefore IT doesn't have to be PROVEN! *"The TRUTH is already TRUE"!* Just remain TRUE to "WHO YOU ARE" and IT'LL tell it for you! The TRUTH will tell on the LIE! So STOP wasting your TIME, ENERGY and BREATHE on THAT and let the TRUTH TELL IT!

Beloveds! You can't CARE or ENTERTAIN the LIES people TELL based off of their TWISTED VIEW! If their VIEW is TWISTED the TRUTH will be TWISTED too! They TELL IT the way they SEE IT! So you can't afford to get CAUGHT UP into what's already TWISTED UP!

Don't be BOUND by BONDAGE! *The 3 Hebrew Boys* in the word of GOD weren't BOUND *(mentally)* even though they were BOUND *(physically)*!

Beloved! The MIRACLE is NOT always what you DON'T have! Sometimes the MIRACLE is what you STILL have! It's WHAT you have LEFT! It's NOT always the THING we're praying, hoping, wishing and believing for; sometimes the MIRACLE is what's REMAINING! The MIRACLE could very well be IN what you ALREADY HAVE!

Listen! This too SHALL PASS! You just got to keep on PASSING in order for it to PASS!

Listen! You can GO THROUGH because GOD SEEN you COME THROUGH! You have to GO THROUGH to COME THROUGH! Besides, this already happened before! Your *NATURAL MAN* is just catching up with what your *SPIRITUAL MAN* has already done! COME THROUGH! You can DO THIS because you already DID IT before!

You have to remember "JESUS already PRAYED you OUT before you went IN"!

Sometimes you have to put your "STEEL TOE" boots on and KICK the devil right in "MIDDLE of IT" and tell him *"That's for all the HELL you put me through while in the MIDDLE of receiving my MIRACLE and my BREAKTHROUGH!* That's for all the FRUSTRATION you caused me while in the MIDDLE of my MEANTIME and BETWEEN TIMES! For all the IMPATIENCE and AGITATION of waiting in the MIDDLE of START to FINISH as though it had not been COMPLETED! This is for all the FEAR and DOUBT brought upon me while trying to TRUST *"ALPHA and OMEGA"* while in the MIDDLE of BEGINNING and END"! Now tell the enemy *"You will not UPSET my JOURNEY nor FRUSTRATE my DESTINY and you will not DELAY my WAIT!*

God is allowing you to *SUPERNATURALLY* survive the CUTBACK without you CUTTING BACK!

You're BELIEVING in a MIRACLE; now make the MIRACLE BELIEVE in YOU!

If GOD has ALL POWER in HIS HANDS and if you're in HIS HANDS then everything pertaining to your *LIFE* is in HIS HANDS too!

EXPECT GOD to DO IT UNEXPECTEDLY and believe HIM to DO the EXPECTED UNEXPECTEDLY!

Your BEST DAYS are not AHEAD of YOU! They are UP-ON YOU!

GOD started with NOTHING and MADE it SOMETHING! Your NOTHING can *BE* your SOMETHING!

There's a difference in the PICTURE of you and the DEPICTION of you! Don't allow people's DEPICTION of you to change the PICTURE of you!

GOD is going to FULLY RESTORE what the enemy tried to DESTROY!

When it RAIN it pours BUT know this, GOD REIGNS over the RAIN!

Just because they are the PEOPLE'S CHOICE doesn't mean they're GOD'S CHOICE!

Some things we call or view as a MIX UP GOD sees it as an opportunity for a HOOK UP! He'll take the MIX UP and use it as a *STEP UP* to HOOK you UP for your next MIRACLE! Some things which seemingly appear to be MESSED UP GOD will use it as a *SET UP* for FAVOR to FIX it UP! Listen, *NOT* all MIXED UP or MESSED UP things are what they seem; some are SET UPs for a STEP UP to your NEXT stream of BLESSINGS!

Don't allow the *DISAPPOINTMENTS* of your PAST to perform an *ERADICATION* to your PRESENT!

Don't allow the *DEVASTATION* of your PAST to become an *EXECUTIONER* to your FUTURE!

Some things were *SUPPOSED* to HAPPEN! It was *"THAT MISERY"* that brought you to *"THIS MIRACLE"! THAT* brought you to *THIS!*

The DECISION you made could've *DESTROYED* you *BUT* the DECISION got *DESTROYED* instead of YOU! #GraceandMercy

Your *OPEN MOUTH* in INTERCESSION can *CLOSE* the *MOUTH* of the enemy's plan and cause an INTERCEPTION to his future plans!

Beloved! While YOU'RE waiting on the NEXT MIRACLE to HAPPEN please know that YOU ARE the NEXT MIRACLE waiting to HAPPEN! You're NOT just waiting on a MIRACLE to HAPPEN! *"YOU ARE* the *MIRACLE"* that's HAPPENING! You're NOT LOOKING for a MIRACLE! MIRACLES are LOOKING for YOU because they're performed by YOU and they are performed for YOU!

God wants YOU to be VALUED by someone who VALUES Your VALUE!

Stay in the FLOW of GOD so you can continue to GLOW in GOD!

YOU are a *"CHANGE AGENT"* now SOUND the alarms for CHANGE! Become the SOUND of CHANGE!

You got to COME THROUGH to COME TO! Going THROUGH brings OUT you! Going THROUGH is what brings you OUT! What's IN you got to come OUT of you! Going THROUGH can bring OUT the *BEST* of YOU or the *WORST* in YOU! What's "IN YOU" will tell "ON YOU" when you're GOING THROUGH! CHARACTER is *BEST BUILT* when GOING THROUGH! IT IS your "GOING THROUGH" that brings you THROUGH! What's bringing you THROUGH is what's bringing you TO! Remember, you don't "GO THROUGH" not to "COME TO" what belongs to you!

Beloved, the only way to LOSE your JOY is to not FIND the presence of The LORD! In HIS PRESENCE there is FULLNESS of JOY and when you're in HIS PRESENCE you'll have HIS JOY! When you have HIS JOY you'll have HIS STRENGTH which gives you the STRENGTH not to LOSE your JOY! When we get IN HIS presence the JOY we thought we once LOST will be FOUND! The moral of this nugget is "YOU CAN'T LOSE IN GOD"!

Your CONFIDENCE will get YOU to the PROMISE if YOU just ENDURE! There's a *GREAT REWARD* for YOU! Your GOING THROUGH is going to REWARD YOU!

Listen, some folk might GET IT FAST but they might LOSE IT QUICK if they didn't go through the PROCESS to KEEP IT! PROCESS helps you KEEP what you GET!

It might take you AWHILE to GET IT but at LEAST you'll GET to KEEP IT once you finally GET IT! PROCESS helps you GET IT but it also helps you KEEP IT!

It might take LONG to GET IT but at least you'll have it LONG when you GET IT! PROCESS provides LONGEVITY to your PROGRESS!

The ADVERSITY that you're going through is ACTUALLY bringing a REWARD to you! There's a *REWARD* for GETTING THROUGH while waiting on GOD to COME THROUGH!

When GOD'S FAVOR is on YOUR LIFE it'll make FOLK have to do YOU a FAVOR! Basically, they have to FAVOR YOU!

Your LAST SEASON is your PAST SEASON so let the *PAST* of that be the *LAST* of that!

Sometimes it's the BREAKDOWN that'll cause you to BREAK OUT! There's a BREAK OUT that's trying to BREAK FORTH in you!

GOD is a PROMISE KEEPER!

Not ONLY does He KEEP His PROMISES but He also KEEPS YOU for the PROMISE! Not ONLY does He KEEP YOU for the PROMISE but He also KEEPS the PROMISE for YOU!

GOD has been KEEPING the PROMISE until HE could TRUST YOU to KEEP IT for YOURSELF!

GOD is NOT looking for PERFECTION! HE expects PROGRESSION!

Just PROGRESS and let God PERFECT!

The STORM doesn't ONLY come to TAKE from you but it ALSO comes to GIVE to you! It *TAKES POWER* but it *GIVES POWER* too! BE the POWER that your STORM produced!

Whenever you find yourself BROKEN you will also find yourself being MADE! The BREAKING is coming to MAKE YOU but DON'T let the MAKING BREAK you!

Your OPPOSITION is taking you to your OPPORTUNITY!

Your TEST is NOT designed to take you OUT but it is designed to take you UP!

You're NOT WAITING on the SUPERNATURAL! You're APART of the SUPERNATURAL!

While you're in the MIDDLE of the WAIT you have to remain PRODUCTIVE while you WAIT! If NOT the enemy of your SOUL will cause you to start *QUESTIONING* your *OWN WAIT!* You have to PRODUCE while you're WAITING for it to be PRODUCED!

VICTORY is NOW! NOW spelled backwards is WON! Therefore, VICTORY is WON NOW and VICTORY is NOW WON!

RESILIENCE is your ability to BOUNCE BACK and to GET BACK what's YOURS! GET UP and GET YOURS! Your GET UP will help you *(to)* GET BACK! It's your GET UP that helps you *(to)* GET ON! Your BOUNCING UP will help you *(to)* BOUNCE BACK! GETTING BACK UP is your *KEY* to GETTING BACK!

The *"NO"* in NO WEAPON means *"NO"* to WEAPONS! You don't have to WORRY about the WEAPON because you got a *"NO"* over your LIFE! The *"NO"* STOPS WEAPONS from prospering in your LIFE!

The enemy CAN'T do NOTHING with a PERSON who knows WHO THEY ARE!

Your TEST had to PROVE that you are APPROVED!

Oftentimes your STRENGTH is found in your WEAKNESS! You're actually *STRONGER* than you *THINK!*

Sometimes it's TOO REAL to *BE TRUE* and HARD to BELIEVE that it can HAPPEN for you AND that you COULD just really WALK THROUGH the DOOR WITHOUT having to actually DO ANYTHING to OPEN the DOOR! You have to *REALIZE* it's because of WHAT you've ALREADY DONE that OPENED the DOOR! Now it's just time to WALK THROUGH *"the DOOR that's OPENED"!* Your last ACT of FAITH, WORSHIP, PRAYER and PRAISE OPENED the DOOR so now you can JUST WALK IN the DOOR!

The BEST of YOU is getting ready to BLESS the REST of YOU! Your *LATTER* shall be *GREATER* than your *FORMER!* The BEST is NOT YET to COME! IT HAS COME! It's ALREADY UP-ON YOU!

You are the MOVEMENT you've been WAITING for!

There are some THINGS that HAVE to HAPPEN simply because it's TIME! It HAS to HAPPEN because it's just YOUR TIME! It HAS to HAPPEN because of the SET TIME! It's already been SET for this TIME!

When it's SET TIME even your "NO" will have to WORK for YOU! Just give it some TIME to reach SET TIME! Your NOW "NO" will become your "YESS" LATER!

Your NO's may have SLAPPED you DOWN but your YES's are getting ready to KNOCK you DOWN!

Your NO's may have SLAPPED you AROUND but your YES's are about to OVERTAKE you by RUNNING you DOWN!

Your NO is SETTING you UP for your YES! Your NO will help you appreciate your YES!

If you give your NO a chance, I promise you IT'LL WORK for you later! As I mentioned before the "NO" you have NOW is becoming your "YES" LATER! It's because of the NO's you received that you are NOW receiving YES's!

Remember, when the *MATURATION* of a "NO" becomes a "YESS" you are getting ready to be TREMENDOUSLY BLESSED!

Those who tried to UNDERESTIMATE you, GOD has OVER ESTIMATED you!

Those that tried to OVERLOOK you, GOD is LOOKING ON you!

You are DESTINED because you've been PREDESTINED! Your DESTINY has been PREDESTINED and has a DESTINATION! You are already DESTINED for your DESTINY! Now YOU ARE just a DESTINY waiting to HAPPEN!

You're ALREADY in your BEFORE! You're ALREADY in what HAPPENED BEFORE! This is ALREADY DONE! You're just WALKING OUT the process of what HAPPENED! YOU are WHAT'S HAPPENING because YOU ALREADY HAPPENED!

Don't SWEAT the small stuff just HANDLE IT!

Be GRATEFUL! There's always another SITUATION that COULD be WORSE than the ONE you're IN right NOW! It could ALWAYS be WORSE but GOD ALWAYS allows US to get the LEAST of the WORST! When you FEEL LIKE you're IN your WORST you're actually IN the BEST of the WORST because the enemy COULDN'T have his way! YES! It could be BETTER but it could also be WORSE! WHAT the enemy tried is NOT what happened! WHAT he wanted to do he COULDN'T do! WHAT he wanted to do COULDN'T WORK because the BLOOD STILL WORKS! Remember it was SUPPOSED to be WORST but it COULDN'T WORK!

Don't get *STUCK* in what HAPPENED that you MISS what's HAPPENING! GET UP and OUT of what HAPPENED and STEP into what's HAPPENING!

If GOD can take the form of a BODY and turn it into SOMEBODY then HE certainly can take your NOTHING and turn it into SOMETHING! Your NOTHING is about to be your SOMETHING!

Your DISAPPOINTMENT is *SETTING you UP* for your DIVINE APPOINTMENT!

Your SETBACK was the STEP BACK to your STEP UP!

Your TROUBLE has POSITIONED you for DOUBLE!

Because you're PREDESTINED the devil is TOO LATE! You're ALREADY in your NEXT! That already HAPPENED! *So what's NEXT!*!

If you feel like you're working with an EMPTY JAR I want to CHALLENGE the way you feel about the JAR being EMPTY! DON'T just look at the EMPTY JAR but look at the FACT that because it's EMPTY it can be FILLED! I SUBMIT to you *TODAY* that your EMPTY JAR can be a FULL JAR! As long as it's EMPTY it could be FILLED! As long as you KEEP the JAR you STILL GOT something to WORK with!

Don't be ASHAMED of your BACKGROUND! GOD will use your BACKGROUND in LIFE to GROUND somebody else BACK in LIFE!

GOD will always CONFIRM what HE AFFIRMED

It's ALRIGHT NOT to BE ALRIGHT! You just NEED to KNOW that you're NOT ALRIGHT in order to get the necessary HELP that you NEED to be ALRIGHT! It's also *OK* not to *KNOW* everything!

YOU have been TRAINED to DEAL with the THING that's trying to DEAL with YOU and TRAINED to HANDLE what's trying to *(have a)* HANDLE *(on)* you! USE it AGAINST it!

Something Else To Consider…

The STORM is over now, so don't *CONFUSE* the effects of the STORM with the STORM!

POINTS TO CONSIDER

7 ENLIGHTENMENT

Ephesians 1:18 | NAS

"I pray that the eyes of your heart may be enlightened, so that you will know what is the hope of His calling, what are the riches of the glory of His inheritance in the saints."

Some of our GREATEST EXPERIENCES in *GOD* were brought on by our EXPERIENCES in LIFE! Some of your WORST ECOUNTERS in LIFE made you EXPERIENCE a LIFE of ENCOUNTERING GOD!

Your PERCEPTION brings about your PERSPECTIVE!

The WAY you SEE IT will result in the WAY you THINK about IT! The WAY you THINK about IT is the WAY you will LIVE BY IT!

SET TIME is when the *PROCESS* of TIME has FULLY been PROCESSED by TIME!

LOOKING BACK is HOLDING us BACK from GOING FORWARD! Always remember the *KEY* to MOVING FORWARD is to STOP GOING BACKWARDS!

An ENCOUNTER with GOD is *NOT* the same as an EXPERIENCE with GOD! Although an ENCOUNTER with GOD should lead us to EXPERIENCE GOD! You can't EXPERIENCE GOD unless you have an EXPERIENCE with GOD and you can't have an EXPERIENCE with GOD unless you EXPERIENCE GOD! Our ENCOUNTERS with GOD should bring us from a *REALIZATION* of GOD to a *REVELATION* about GOD by way of EXPERIENCE with GOD! An ENCOUNTER represents a MEETING with GOD but an EXPERIENCE represents an OCCURRENCE with GOD! Not ONLY are we MEETING HIM but something HAPPENS when we MEET HIM!

BLINDERS will HINDER you from SEEING and will BLOCK your VIEW but the SCALES of DECEPTION will STOP you from SEEING what's really TRUE!

Some TRANSPARENCY is just a justification for CARNALITY!

Some "I'm JUST KEEPING it REAL" is really a warning for "I'm ABOUT to BE in MY FLESH"! #RealTalk

We become the WORDS that we SPEAK! As THOUGHTS utter WORDS, WORDS utters ACTIONS, ACTIONS utters HABITS, HABITS utters CHARACTER and CHARACTER utters YOU! Watch your SPEECH they can become YOU!

Your PERSECUTION speaks of your IMPACT! LOW IMPACT = LOW PERSECUTION!

CARING folk need someone to CARE for them TOO!

Just because someone is CARING don't OVERLOOK the fact that they NEED to be *CARED* for too! WE can't just CARE about the NEED they have to CARE for another without CARING for their NEEDS too!

STRONG people need STRENGTH TOO!

Just because someone is STRONG and possesses *STRENGTH* to you, doesn't mean they're NEVER WEAK and NEVER looking for someone else to be STRONG for them too"!

The "To GO To" person NEEDS someone "To GO To" TOO!

Just because a person is the "To GO To" person or in some eyes "The HELP" doesn't mean they don't *NEED HELP!* Don't make the mistake of mistaking them as NEVER needing "To GO To" someone for HELP!

We have to be sensitive and PAY ATTENTION because *THEY, WE, ME, YOU* "NEED" TOO!

Just because we're doing "SPIRITUAL THINGS" doesn't mean we're doing those THINGS in the SPIRIT of GOD!

Just because we're doing "SPIRITUAL THINGS" doesn't mean we're automatically SPIRITUAL nor does it mean we're in THE SPIRIT!

There's a difference in being CAUTIOUS and STANDOFFISH!

Some BETRAYALS didn't have to be BETRAYAL had NOT we BETRAYED what we KNEW and what GOD SHOWED us! We STILL made the DECISION to get INVOLVED! In retrospect AND as a result in MANY instances we BETRAYED ourselves because we DIDN'T LISTEN to our INNER self!

You don't have to worry about it being GOOD when it's GOD! When it's GOD it's GOOD!

Don't confuse GOOD with GOOD ENOUGH! IT'LL never be GOOD ENOUGH!

Simply put...

Don't settle for GOOD ENOUGH when you can have GOOD!

Remember, the POWER comes BACK ON after the STORM! BUT also remember we can learn VALUABLE LESSONS while in the STORM if we allow the STORM to teach us! We don't have to *WAIT* to receive POWER afterwards when we can receive POWER while in it!

We're MISSING IT because we WON'T GET IT!

In other words...

We're MISSING what GOD HAS for us because we WON'T LISTEN to what GOD TOLD us!

FAITH IS what *YOU SAW* not what YOU SEE! We have to SEE IT and BELIEVE IT spiritually by ENVISIONING IT in the spirit and RECEIVING IT by FAITH! We have to SPEAK IT naturally by UTTERING IT verbally and ACCEPT IT physically into our existence!

Are you trying to figure out whether you're DOING IT for YOU or for THEM? When you're doing IT for YOU, SELF will always be the INDICATION of the MOTIVATION! SELF GRATIFICATION will always let you know whether your *MOTIVES* are pure for doing what YOU do because SELF will always seek SATISFACTION and YOU will always be the CENTER of IT! That's how YOU know you're DOING IT for YOU! IT will always PLEASE YOU and not THEM!

Some are OBEDIENT but NOT SUBMITTED! One of the reasons we find it hard to *RESIST* the enemy is because we won't *SUBMIT* to GOD!

Be careful not to MISTAKE or MISUNDERSTAND FRUSTRATION! In some cases a state of FRUSTRATION is a condition caused by a *LACK of FULFILMENT!* It's characterized as *ANNOYANCE* due to UNFULFILLMENT! It can become a *VEXATION* due to NONFULFILLMENT and an INDICATOR that things aren't COMPLETE! There may be a sense of *DISAPPOINTMENT* and *DISSATISFACTION* when things are UNFULFILLED and as a result you are NOT FULFILLED! There's a REACTION when things are STAGNANT, HINDERED and just at a STAND STILL making it impossible for things to be FULFILLED! Sometimes we are FRUSTRATED because there are things we haven't ACCOMPLISHED or DONE and if we can honestly admit sometimes *"We're really FRUSTRATED with US and because of US"!*

There are just some things we STILL have to *DO* in order to FULFILL what we're CALLED to DO!

HUSTLING ain't FAITH! Just because we *GRIND* to GET IT, don't mean GOD GAVE IT!

DENIAL ain't FAITH! Refusing to *BELIEVE IT* doesn't mean we BELIEVE GOD!

STUBBORNNESS ain't FAITH! Just because you DON'T BELIEVE GOD said *MOVE* doesn't mean GOD DIDN'T say MOVE!

Being AMBITIOUS ain't FAITH! Just because you're *DRIVEN* to IT, doesn't mean GOD DROVE you to IT! Being DRIVEN doesn't mean GOD is *(doing the)* DRIVING!

FALLING SHORT is not the same a PREMEDITATED FALLING!

People will try to UNDERESTIMATE you when you're not *ARROGANT* about you! You know WHO you are; you're just not PRIDEFUL about it! There's a difference in *CONFIDENCE and COOKINESS!* CONFIDENCE is "KNOWING WHO YOU ARE"! COCKINESS is "BEING *ARROGANT* about WHO YOU ARE"!

Sometimes we can't be HEALED because we won't be REAL! Be REAL to be HEALED!

Sometimes the BEST CHANGE ever made is *TELLING* the TRUTH! TRUTH is synonymous with CHANGE!

A LIFE *of PRAYER* is a STYLE *of LIFE* turned into a LIFESTYLE *of PRAYER!* Beloveds PRAYER is a LIFESTYLE!

GOD shall DELIVER but HOW are you GONNA HANDLE the DELIVERY?

There's a difference between HEARING and ADHERING! We might *HEAR* GOD but we also need to *ADHERE* to GOD!

When our LOVE for GOD supersedes our LOVE for ourselves living HOLY comes EASY!

When our LOVE for GOD surpasses our LOVE for the WORLD obeying GOD'S WORD comes EASY!

When our LOVE for GOD transcends our LOVE for our OWN WILL, WANTS and DESIRES then GOD'S WILL becomes EASY to us!

When our LOVE for GOD exceeds our LOVE for DOING what we want, DOING what GOD wants comes EASY!

When our LOVE for GOD excels our LOVE for our POSSESSIONS, GIVING back to GOD what HE put in our POSSESSION comes EASY!

When our LOVE for GOD goes beyond our LOVE for our JOBS *"Our Resource"* TRUSTING GOD *"The Ultimate Source"* comes EASY!

When our LOVE for GOD overpasses our LOVE for POPULAR APPROVAL being APPROVING to GOD comes EASY!

When our LOVE for GOD trumps our LOVE for THAT putting GOD first comes EASY!

When our LOVE for GOD beats the LOVE we have for SELF the LOVE for the THINGS of GOD becomes EASY!

Our INTENTIONS might be one thing but our ACTIONS are another! If NOT CAREFUL your *ACTIONS* will become your *INTENTIONS!* If you KEEP DOING IT you NOW INTEND to DO IT!

No ONE makes a MISTAKE on PURPOSE but when ONE continuously makes that MISTAKE, that MISTAKE could now be considered as made on PURPOSE by that ONE! If you CONTINUE IT now IT becomes IT! Your CONTINUAL will become IT if you CONTINUE to DO IT! *ALSO* the thing you CONTINUE to DO is the thing that *BECOMES* you!

INFORMATION is normally *STORED* based off of its IMPORTANCE to us! We remember what's IMPORTANT to us!

There's a thin line between FAITH and FOLLY! FOLLY is when we try to RATIONALIZE IT as FAITH because we didn't *"COUNT up the COST"!* We then try to CONVINCE ourselves IT was FAITH because *"FAITH without WORKS is DEAD".* Now if I could, I would like to submit that WORKS without FAITH that are done with FOLLY is already DEAD! *"The BLESSINGS of The LORD makes RICH and ADD NO SORROW with IT".* FAITH will be MARKED by BLESSINGS and FOLLY will be MARKED by SORROW!

FAITH or FOLLY? FAITH will be MARKED by PEACE even if IT'S AGAINST ALL ODDS! FOLLY will be MARKED by PRESSURE because the ODDS are STACKED UP AGAINST you!

FAITH or FOLLY? FAITH causes you to MOVE with URGENCY and because of the URGENCY! FOLLY will cause you to MOVE because of PRESSURE and from being PRESSURED! There's a DIFFERENCE in URGENCY and PRESSURE!

FAITH or FOLLY? FAITH will cause you to MOVE because of GOD'S AGENDA! FOLLY will cause you to MOVE because of a PERSONAL or HIDDEN AGENDA!

FAITH can only APPROPIATE what GOD DELIBERATES!

ENDURE to MATURE! Some things don't COME UP until we GROW UP! They don't COME until we MATURE! We have to learn to ENDURE in order to MATURE!

Sometimes we're NOT just dealing with *"The ISSUE"* we're dealing with *"The TRIGGER"* of the ISSUE! ANGER, HURTS and PAINS that are unresolved will begin to *TARGET* a *TRIGGER* for you! This person will be stepping into the *CROSSFIRE* of something that didn't even *START* with them! When this happens we are making them PAY for what they DIDN'T do!

It's called GENUINE LOVE and that's what IT DOES! IT LOVES and it makes others LOVE YOU while others are CONFUSED about why they LOVE YOU and UPSET because they LOVE YOU! It's hard for a person to comprehend what's not GENUINELY in them!

The enemy is not FOCUSED on your OPPOSITION! He's FOCUSED on your OPPORTUNITY! He uses OPPOSITIONS to *DISTRACT* you from the OPPORTUNITY! He can CARE LESS about what you're GOING THROUGH he CARES MORE about what you're GOING TO! He's just using your OPPOSITION to *DISTRACT* you while he tries to *SABOTAGE* your OPPORTUNITY! #StayFOCUSED

There's a difference in TRUSTING GOD when you have MONEY and TRUSTING GOD with your MONEY! It's easy to TRUST Him WITH it but try TRUSTING Him WITHOUT it!

The ONLY PURPOSE the PAST had was to FORM you and to BIRTH OUT the NEW you!

The ONLY OPPORTUNITY the enemy GETS is the OPPORTUNITY we GIVE! STOP GIVING and he won't GET IT!

Just because *THEY* didn't HEAR YOU doesn't mean *YOU* didn't SAY IT! Just KEEP SPEAKING someone will HEAR and RECEIVE IT!

Just because you ALREADY TRIED don't mean you have to GIVE UP NOW! Don't STOP TRYING because you TRIED!

Just because the enemy TALKS to YOU don't mean YOU have to TALK to him! Don't LISTEN!

Just because the enemy KNOCKS on your DOOR don't mean you have to OPEN the DOOR! Keep it CLOSED!

PERCEPTION is *HOW* you SEE! PERSPECTIVE is *HOW* you THINK about WHAT you SEE!

Our CURRENT VIEW could be *INTERFERING* with our CLEAR VIEW! Sometimes we have to LOOK AGAIN!

If we can ONLY SEE WHAT we're *SEEING* then we're NOT SEEING at ALL!

WHAT we SEE is different from *HOW* we SEE! Sometimes we have to ask ourselves "HOW DO I SEE WHAT I SEE"?

We have to have VISION to have VISION! Sometimes GOD has to put HIS SUPER on OUR NATURAL!

JEALOUSY is an EVIL THING! It will DECEIVE you and make you think you're NOT JEALOUS at ALL while that's ALL OTHERS can SEE! Jealousy + Pride = Danger!

We can RECEIVE, ACHIEVE, ASSERTAIN and SUCCEED in many things but are we able to KEEP, MAINTAIN and SUSTAIN them? CHARACTER plays an INTEGRAL role in these things! Our INTEGRITY, CHARACTER and REPUTATION means everything to the LIFE, LONGEVITY and SUCCESS of ALL things RECEIVED!

Let's Talk Character and Reputation Again…

CHARACTER is WHAT YOU DO! REPUTATION is WHAT they SAY about YOU based off of WHAT YOU DO!

CHARACTER is not WHAT they SAID about YOU! It's WHAT YOU SAY about YOU based off of WHAT YOU DO! IT is YOU because of WHAT YOU continue to DO!

Your REPUTATION is WHAT'S TOLD! Your CHARACTER is WHAT TELLS! Your REPUTATION is based off of your "SHOW and TELL"! Your CHARACTER SHOWS them what to TELL! Your CHARACTER "SHOWED" and your REPUTATION "TOLD"! Your CHARACTER is WHAT YOU continue TO DO so now your REPUTATION TOLD on YOU!

It's not WHAT you SAID! It's HOW you SAID IT! Don't let your DELIVERY mess up your MESSAGE!

People SECRETLY ENVY you because you're BOLD ENOUGH to DO what they WON'T DO!

The SITUATION is *NOT* really a *SITUATION* because GOD has already SITUATED it!

It's HARD to get SOMEWHERE when you don't know WHERE you're COMING from! Even the NAVIGATION can't TAKE you "THERE" without knowing "WHERE" you are! It's ESSENTIAL to know your START POINT to get to your END POINT! It's VITAL to know WHERE you ARE to know WHERE you're GOING! The GPS and NAVIGATION has to know your "CURRENT LOCATION" to get you to your "DESTINATION"! It can't TAKE you NOWHERE unless it knows WHERE you're GOING and WHERE you're COMING from! As it is in the NATURAL so it is in the SPIRIT!

Don't be surprised if there's a DIVINE CONNECTION by way of a DIVINE DISCONNECTION!

GOD has to SHOW you IT so you can start HOPING for IT! HOPE is BELIEVING something *DESIRED* could be HAD! NOW your FAITH wants to bring that BELIEF to PASS!

When you DON'T PAY the enemy any ATTENTION he then has to LEAVE to GET ATTENTION! He has to GO GET ATTENTION from someone that will PAY him ATTENTION because ATTENTION is what he needs!

Your TRUTH will CHANGE your LIFE! Your TRUTH will give you an EXCHANGE for a BETTER LIFE! Your ONE TRUTH can CHANGE your LIFE as well as somebody else's LIFE and IT can give them a much BETTER LIFE!

One Last Reflection…

Sometimes there needs to be "EXPOSURE to bring forth CLOSURE"

MY REFLECTIONS

8 STOP LETTING

"Stop letting people who do so little for you control so much of your mind, feelings and emotions."

- Will Smith-

STOP LETTING people PUMP you UP who want to see you LET DOWN!

STOP LETTING people that TALK ABOUT you TALK TO you! When you TALK to THEM they can't wait to TALK to THEM!

STOP LETTING people MAKE PROMISES who couldn't KEEP the last PROMISE and have NO plans of KEEPING the next PROMISE!

PS. It looks very PROMISING that they can't keep PROMISES!

STOP LETTING people try to BIND you to what they're BOUND to!

STOP LETTING people PRETEND to LIKE you and you KNOW they DON'T LIKE you! LOVE them BUT let them KNOW "I SEE YOU"!

STOP LETTING people try to DOWN PLAY what you said by trying to PLAY UP what SOMEBODY else said and you BOTH said the SAME THING! DON'T let them *(try to)* DEVALUE your VALUE!

STOP LETTING people *(try to)* DUMB you DOWN *(just)* to PUMP themselves UP!

STOP LETTING people TELL you "WHAT GOD SAID" but you SEE "NO GODLY FRUIT" in their lives!

STOP LETTING people who've DIGRESSED come against your PROGRESS!

STOP LETTING people think because you "DON'T SAY NOTHING" that you "DON'T KNOW NOTHING"! LET them KNOW you KNOW!

STOP LETTING people TELL you WHAT to DO that never had to DO IT or have never done anything remotely CLOSE to IT!

STOP LETTING people COME to USE YOU but won't COME to HELP YOU!

STOP LETTING people make you PAY for WHAT you DIDN'T DO! Trying to make you PAY for WHAT DIDN'T START with you and now you're CAUGHT UP in the CROSSFIRE of their MESS and you DON'T even know WHAT to do with the MESS!

STOP LETTING people TELL you they LOVE you but DON'T ever SHOW you!

STOP LETTING folk think they FOOLED you, when in actuality they are a FOOL for trying to FOOL you!

STOP LETTING folk "TRICK" you whose CHARACTER already tells you that they are a "TRICKSTER"!

STOP LETTING people TELL you ONE THING and their ACTIONS SHOW ANOTHER and because of their CHARACTER they will still try to CONVINCE you of the THING they tried to TELL you!

PASTORS! STOP LETTING your CHURCH MEMBERS put the PRESS on you about being a "GOOD PASTOR" but they won't be a "GOOD MEMBER"!

STOP LETTING people LIE to you and you KNOW they're LYING to you!

STOP LETTING people TALK AT you but won't TALK TO you!

STOP LETTING people UNDERESTIMATE you because they want to OVERESTIMATE themselves!

STOP LETTING people COME to YOU *(just)* to COME through YOU to GET to SOMEONE ELSE and now *(they)* FORGET about YOU!

STOP LETTING people FOOL you and let their CHARACTER TELL you!

STOP LETTING people SECRETLY ACKNOWLEDGE you but won't OPENLY RECOGNIZE you!

STOP LETTING people make you FEEL LIKE you've done SOMETHING to *(victimize)* them because you WON'T let them do SOMETHING to *(victimize)* you!

STOP LETTING folk TALK you OUT of a GOOD EXPERIENCE because they had a BAD EXPERIENCE!

STOP LETTING people LEAD you that CAN'T FOLLOW their own LEAD!

STOP LETTING people SPEAK in your LIFE that DON'T allow GOD to SPEAK to them ABOUT their LIFE!

STOP LETTING folk SCARE YOU out of things because they allowed FEAR to SCARE THEM out of it!

STOP LETTING folk MINISTER to you that "DESPERATELY" need to be MINISTERED to!

STOP LETTING FOLK take YOU through the "FRIEND TEST" TESTING your loyalty! TESTING your commitment! TESTING your trustworthiness! TESTING your confidentiality! TESTING your ability to support and be there for them but they're FAILING "ALL" the "SAME" TEST they're putting you through! STOP IT...DON'T let them DO IT to YOU! If THEY can EXPECT it from YOU then YOU should be able to EXPECT it from THEM! YES they have to properly VET you but they don't have to keep TESTING you!

List some of your personal STOP LET'S as a NOTE to SELF...

STOP LETTING

9 I'M CONVINCED

"When people show you who they are believe them."

-Dr. Maya Angelou-

I'm CONVINCED that when a person shows me WHO they are, I don't need to SEE NO MORE because I already BELIEVE them!

I'm CONVINCED that you should be very CAUTIOUS and LEARY of people who want to PRIVATELY ACKNOWLEDGE you but won't PUBLICALLY RECOGNIZE you!

I'm CONVINCED that some people still don't REALIZE the CONSTANT TROUBLES they're having have much to do with the CONSTANT WRONGS they've done!

I'm CONVINCED that some are confusing PUSHING a DOOR OPEN as the same as GOD OPENING the DOOR!

I'm CONVINCED that some are confusing RUBBING SHOULDERS with GOD'S FAVOR!

I'm CONVINCED that some people have the tendencies of telling HALF TRUTHS so you can believe their TRUTH without knowing the WHOLE TRUTH!

I'm CONVINCED that some folk will try to CALL others MESSY, all because they EXPOSED their MESS! They will ALWAYS try to make it LOOK LIKE IT'S YOU because YOU know the TRUTH!

I'm CONVINCED we want to operate in The GIFTS *(abilities and acts)* of the SPIRIT without the FRUIT *(characteristics and nature)* of the SPIRIT!

I'm CONVINCED that operating in the GIFTS "Charisma" of the SPIRIT without operating in the FRUIT of the SPIRIT equals the works of THE FLESH!

I'm CONVINCED that SPIRITUAL GIFTS without MATURITY = MISAPPROPIATED POWER!

I'm CONVINCED that if our ONLY source of INFORMATION is what somebody TOLD us then we CANNOT VERIFY that that INFORMATION is TRUE!

I'm CONVINCED that some things are MISPLACED and DISPLACED in our lives because we're OUT of PLACE and refuse to GET in PLACE!

I'm CONVINCED that it's just too much WORK to PRETEND when it's not NECCESSARY or WORTH it!

I'm CONVINCED that some things are a SAD REALITY but a REAL REALITY!

I'm CONVINCED that some folk are not really CELEBRATING YOU; they're just there to FIGURE OUT the DOOR you just came THROUGH! They're not there to HELP and SUPPORT YOU, they're there CHECKING IT OUT to see if they can come THROUGH the same DOOR you just went THROUGH! They are not there to WATCH you be CELEBRATED; they're WATCHING the DOOR that's CELEBRATING you!

I'm CONVINCED that FAKE CELEBRATORS always want to be CELEBRATED during your CELEBRATION! Beware of those who seek to be CELEBRATED while you're being CELEBRATED!

I'm CONVINCED that some people will ALWAYS have to DISAGREE, MURMUR, COMPLAIN and not LIKE what you're DOING because everybody CAN'T GO where you're GOING! There WILL always be some NO's because SOMEBODY have to BE the ONES to WATCH the TABLE be PREPARED for YOU!

I'm CONVINCED that some people's NATURAL ability to SEE and HEAR will NOT be able to PERCEIVE nor CONCEIVE what GOD has in STORE for YOU! #WatchGod

I'm CONVINCED that people LOVE YOU until you START DEALING with those THINGS they thought they could HIDE from you!

I'm CONVINCED that if we are not CAREFUL we can easily turn experiences intended to be SPIRITUAL into a RITUAL or a RELIGIOUS ACT if we do not maintain the SIGNIFICANCE of it! SIGNIFICANCE is *"the QUALITY of being SIGNIFICANT or having a MEANING"* translated…let's keep the MAIN THING the MAIN THING!

I'm CONVINCED that if a person doesn't ALLOW GOD to do something with THEM certainly YOU can't do nothing with them but PRAY for them; continue to LOVE them and KEEP IT MOVING! If they can't be MOVED by GOD, you certainly can't MOVE 'em but you can REMOVE them and yourself by KEEPING IT MOVING!

I'm CONVINCED that IT may NOT be your TURN but IT'S definitely your TIME! GOD is NOT concerned about "WHO'S TURN IT IS" but rather "WHO'S TIME IT IS"! When it's YOUR TIME! TURN won't matter!

I'm CONVINCED that what you DON'T DEAL with NOW, you will have to DEAL with LATER!

I'm CONVINCED that many have been taught to be GREAT on the OUTSIDE but GOD desires to teach us how to be GREAT from the INSIDE OUT!

I'm CONVINCED that some people will APOLOGIZE to you but will never GO BACK and CLEAN UP the MESS they made about you! They will PRIVATELY apologize but won't PUBLICALLY go back to those they told the LIE to!

I'm CONVINCED that some are FALLING by the WAYSIDE but LOOKING GOOD on the OUTSIDE!

I'm CONVINCED that people who KNOW other people THROUGH you but PRETEND not to KNOW you are QUESTIONABLE people!

I'm CONVINCED that people who DISCONNECT from you but SECRETLY establish CONNECTIONS through you are DISLOYAL people and not TRUSTWORTHY!

I'm CONVINCED that people who develop RELATIONSHIPS through you but NOW show no RELATIONS to you are not to be regarded as an AUTHENTIC RELATIONSHIP!

I'm CONVINCED that some people don't LIKE you but they LIKE who you are CONNECTED to, therefore they PRETEND to LIKE you just to CONNECT with those CONNECTED to you!

I'm CONVINCED that there's something seriously wrong when people say they're with YOU *(privately)* but they are with EVERYBODY ELSE *(publicly)* except YOU!

I'm CONVINCED that you can't be LOYAL to BOTH because eventually you will HAVE to be DISLOYAL to ONE! These types of friendships should be regarded as PART TIME or relationships of CONVENIENCE!

I'm CONVINCED there's a difference in GETTING OVER something and getting PAST IT! You can GET OVER IT but it doesn't mean you have MOVED ON from it! When you get PAST IT it's behind you and you're able to MOVE ON from IT!

I'm CONVINCED that BLINDERS BLOCK your VIEW, but DECEPTION STOPS you from seeing the TRUTH!

I'm CONVINCED that people DON'T WANT YOU until they NEED YOU! Don't get UPSET it's just human nature!

I'm CONVINCED that some things we can't take so SERIOUSLY! LIFE is TOO SHORT! People will be People! We have to LEARN to LAUGH things OFF! Some things are to be expected because it's just HUMAN NATURE! When WE learn to LAUGH at things that are TOO LOW for us is when we can truly say we can "LIVE, LAUGH & LOVE"!

I'm CONVINCED that some people are ALL RIGHT with *(their)* WRONG!

I'm CONVINCED that some people who use LIP SERVICE to "SAY" they are with you actually "SHOW" you through their ACTIONS and DEEDS that they are INDEED NOT with you!

I'm CONVINCED that when some people CAN'T get their WAY they will try to ASSASSINATE your CHARACTER, SABOTAGE your NAME and LIE on YOU simply because you won't let THEM DO what THEY want to DO! Sometimes you have to tell folk "You can LIE and SABOTAGE all you want, I'M NOT letting YOU have your WAY" #IJS

I'm CONVINCED that folk who try to "USE YOU" will try to turn it around like they're being "MISUSED by YOU! Sometimes you just have to tell folk "I'm not going to let you USE ME and I'm not going to MISUSE YOU" #IJS

I'm CONVINCED that some people act like you're doing something WRONG to THEM all because you WON'T let THEM do something WRONG to YOU! Sometimes you have to tell people "I did NO WRONG to YOU but I'M NOT letting YOU do ME WRONG" #IJS

I'm CONVINCED that some FOLK will act like YOU'RE doing something to THEM all because YOU WON'T let THEM do something to YOU! Sometimes you just have to tell folk "I'm NOT doing NOTHING to YOU and I'M NOT letting YOU do NOTHING to ME" #IJS

I'm CONVINCED that some people don't like YOU to say NO to THEM and then try to ACT like you've WRONGED them by saying NO to THEM! Sometimes you just have to tell folk "I did nothing WRONG to YOU but I'M NOT going to let YOU do nothing WRONG ME" #IJS

I'm CONVINCED that YOU have to "STAND UP" in WHO YOU ARE so WHO YOU ARE can "STAND OUT"!

I'm CONVINCED that some people shouldn't TALK ABOUT what they DON'T UNDERSTAND!

I'm CONVINCED that some folk don't LIKE YOU because YOU LIKE YOU and others LIKE YOU too!

I'm CONVINCED that some folk MISTAKE MEEKNESS for WEAKNESS!

I'm CONVINCED that some people think just because you're GODLY means you're GULLIBLE!

I'm CONVINCED that some people don't even REALIZE they're COMPETING with YOU all because of their JEALOUSY towards YOU!

I'm CONVINCED that acceptance, confession and real repentance brings forth TRUE DELIVERANCE!

I'm CONVINCED that when you START TELLING on them, they'll STOP TELLING it to you! Your START TELLING will STOP them from TELLING!

I'm CONVINCED that people with TRUST ISSUES will always LOOK for a REASON not to TRUST you!

I'm CONVINCED that some people will never figure out WHY they have CYCLES in their lives because they've been TALKING about you ALL their LIVES!

I'm CONVINCED that some things people call STRATEGIES or consider as STRATEGIC is really called MANIPULATION and being MANIPULATIVE!

I'm CONVINCED that every person who has a TRUE RELATIONSHIP with GOD shouldn't have to WAIT for several people to TELL them that there's a need to make some CHANGES in their LIVES!

I'm CONVINCED that you don't ALWAYS have to DO something DIFFERENT to make a DIFFERENCE! Sometimes you just need to BE the DIFFERENCE! That alone will make a DIFFERENCE!

I'm CONVINCED that JEALOUSY is an EVIL THING! It will DECEIVE YOU and make YOU THINK you're NOT JEALOUS at ALL when that's ALL OTHERS can SEE about YOU! Jealousy + Pride = Danger!

I'm CONVINCED that some people will USE YOU to get WHAT they WANT from YOU and can CARE LESS about YOU!

I'm CONVINCED that there are some DIVINE CONNECTIONS established even if it is through the DISCONNECTED!

I'm CONVINCED that we have GROWN so SOCIAL MEDIA driven that we have become ANTI SOCIAL!

I'm CONVINCED that TECHNOLOGY *(text, inbox, email & DM)* is the new way to CONFRONT ISSUES without actually having to COME IN FRONT of the PERSON we actually have the ISSUE with!

I'm CONVINCED that LOYALTY means NOTHING to some people when AMBITIONS and PERSONAL GAIN is their AIM!

I'm CONVINCED you can ALWAYS tell WHO'S been TALKING to WHOM because now they don't TALK to YOU!

I'm CONVINCED that even your JUDAS will have to COME BACK to BLESS YOU!

I'm CONVINCED that the ONLY OPPORTUNITY the enemy GETS is the OPPORTUNITY we GIVE!

I'm CONVINCED that some people CAN'T HANDLE you being you but prefer you to CHANGE to accommodate what they can HANDLE about you! They would prefer a FAKE you simply because they're not READY for the REAL you! BE YOU whether they can HANDLE YOU or NOT!

I'm CONVINCED that there are some things that are supposed to HAPPEN and some things that have to HAPPEN! It's just a part of our DESTINY! That's IT and that's ALL!

I'm CONVINCED that you should BE CAREFUL of people who in ONE MINUTE you're the BEST THING since SLICED BREAD and the NEXT MINUTE someone else IS and now you're the WORST THING since you SLICED into their BREAD! It speaks much of their CHARACTER! It's WHAT they DO! If they DO IT to YOU more than likely they WILL DO IT to them TOO! They also DID IT to others before they DID IT to you! Be WISE and Open your EYES!

I'm CONVINCED that sometimes you may have to let people know that "I know your HEART is not PURE towards me, I just SMILE and STILL LOVE you but DON'T THINK I'm FOOLED by you! I SEE YOU!

I'm CONVINCED that FAMILIARITY breeds DISHONOR and spawns DISRESPECT!

I'm CONVINCED that we have to EXPERIENCE a FEW things just to understand SOME things!

I'm CONVINCED that when people LIE ON you that you should just let the people they LIED to WATCH the FRUIT and they'll soon SEE who's the LIAR and who's the TRUTH! You can't CHASE DOWN every LIE! The LIE and the LIAR will soon have to TELL the TRUTH because FRUIT don't LIE! It produces after IT'S OWN KIND! Get some REST and let the TRUTH handle the REST!

I'm CONVINCED that if we can't HONOR GOD we certainly can't HONOR the MAN or WOMAN of GOD! The way we REVERE and RELATE to GOD's set MAN and WOMAN of GOD is an indicator of our REVERENCE and RELATIONSHIP with GOD!

I'm also CONVINCED that the way we TREAT PEOPLE is the way we TREAT GOD! Our RELATIONSHIP with PEOPLE on the earth realm speaks directly to our RELATIONSHIP with GOD in the spiritual realm!

List some things you are CONVINCED about as a NOTE to SELF...

I'M CONVINCED

SCRIPTURES

WISDOM

James 1:5 | NAS

But if any of you lacks wisdom, let him ask of God, who gives to all generously and without reproach, and it will be given to him.

Proverbs 2:6 | KJV

For the Lord giveth wisdom Out of his mouth cometh knowledge and understanding.

Proverbs 16:16 | KJV

How much better is it to get wisdom than gold! And to get understanding rather to be chosen than silver!

Proverbs 2:6 | NAS

For the LORD gives wisdom; From His mouth come knowledge and understanding.

Proverbs 13:10 | KJV

Only by pride cometh contention but with the well advised is wisdom.

Proverbs 19:8 | KJV

He that getteth wisdom loveth his own soul he that keepeth understanding shall find good.

Matthew 7:24 | KJV

Therefore whosoever heareth these sayings of mine, and doeth them, I will liken him unto a wise man, which built his house upon a rock.

Proverbs 15:33 | KJV

The fear of the Lord is the instruction of wisdom; and before honour is humility.

Proverbs 3:13 | KJV

Happy is the man that findeth wisdom, and the man that getteth understanding.

Proverbs 4:11 | KJV

I have taught thee in the way of wisdom; I have led thee in right paths.

Proverbs 4:5 | KJV

Get wisdom, get understanding: forget it not; Neither decline from the words of my mouth.

Ecclesiastes 10:12 | KJV

The words of a wise man's mouth are gracious; But the lips of a fool will swallow up himself.

Proverbs 1:7 | KJV

The fear of the Lord is the beginning of knowledge but fools despise wisdom and instruction.

Proverbs 4:7 | KJV

Wisdom is the principal thing; therefore get wisdom: And with all thy getting get understanding.

Ephesians 1:17 | KJV

That the God of our Lord Jesus Christ, the Father of glory, may give unto you the spirit of wisdom and revelation in the knowledge of him.

Proverbs 10:31 MSG

A good person's mouth is a clear fountain of wisdom; a foul mouth is a stagnant swamp.

INSIGHT

Proverbs 2:3 |AMP

Yes, if you cry out for insight, and lift up your voice for understanding;

Ephesians 1:8 |AMP

Which He lavished on us. In all wisdom and understanding [with practical insight].

Proverbs 1:2 | AMP

To know [skillful and godly] wisdom and instruction; to discern and comprehend the words of understanding and insight,

Proverbs 9:6 | AMP

"Leave [behind] your foolishness [and the foolish] and live, and walk in the way of insight and understanding."

John 8:27 | AMP

They did not realize [or have the spiritual insight to understand] that He was speaking to them about the Father.

2 Corinthians 6:6 | AMP

In purity and sincerity, in knowledge and spiritual insight, in patience, in kindness, in the Holy Spirit, in genuine love,

Ephesians 3:4 | AMP

By referring to this, when you read it you can understand my insight into the mystery of Christ,

Proverbs 3:5 | AMP

Trust in and rely confidently on the Lord with all your heart and do not rely on your own insight or understanding.

Psalm 119:99 | AMP

I have better understanding and deeper insight than all my teachers [because of your word], For Your testimonies are my meditation.

Proverbs 12:8 | AMP

A man will be commended according to his insight and sound judgment, but the one who is of a perverse mind will be despised.

Proverbs 16:22 | AMP

Understanding (spiritual insight) is a [refreshing and boundless] wellspring of life to those who have it, But to give instruction and correction to fools is foolishness.

Daniel 9:22 | AMP

He instructed me and he talked with me and said, "O Daniel, I have now come to give you insight and wisdom and understanding.

Luke 6:11 | AMP

But the scribes and Pharisees were filled with senseless rage [and lacked spiritual insight], and discussed with one another what they might do to Jesus.

1 Corinthians 1:5 | AMP

so that in everything you were [exceedingly] enriched in Him, in all speech [empowered by the spiritual gifts] and in all knowledge [with insight into the faith].

INSPIRATIONS

2 Timothy 3:16 | KJV

All scripture [is] given by inspiration of God, and [is] profitable for doctrine, for reproof, for correction, for instruction in righteousness,

Mathew 22:43 | AMP

Jesus asked them, "How is it then that David by the inspiration of the Spirit, calls Him 'Lord,' saying,

Ezekiel 13:2 | AMP

"Son of man, prophesy against the prophets of Israel who prophesy, and say to those who prophesy from their own inspiration, 'Hear the word of the Lord!

Ezekiel 13:17 | AMP

"Now you, son of man, set your face against the daughters of your people who are prophesying out of [the wishful thinking of] their own mind (inspiration). Prophesy against them.

Acts 6:10 | AMP

But they were not able to successfully withstand and cope with the wisdom and the intelligence [and the power and inspiration] of the Spirit by whom he was speaking.

Job 32:8 | AMP

But there is [a vital force and] a spirit [of intelligence] in man, and the breath of the Almighty gives them understanding.

2 Peter 1:20 | AMP

But understand this first of all, that no prophecy of Scripture is a matter of or comes from one's own [personal or special] interpretation,

John 16:13 | KJV

Howbeit when he, the Spirit of truth, is come, he will guide you into all truth: for he shall not speak of himself; but whatsoever he shall hear, [that] shall he speak: and he will shew you things to come.

Job 32:8 | KJV

But [there is] a spirit in man: and the inspiration of the Almighty giveth them understanding.

John 14:26 | KJV

But the Comforter, [which is] the Holy Ghost, whom the Father will send in my name, he shall teach you all things, and bring all things to your remembrance, whatsoever I have said unto you.

2 Peter 1:21 | KJV

For the prophecy came not in old time by the will of man: but holy men of God spake [as they were] moved by the Holy Ghost.

ILLUMINATION

1 Corinthians 12:7 | AMP

But to each one is given the manifestation of the Spirit [the spiritual illumination and the enabling of the Holy Spirit] for the common good.

Genesis 1:3 | AMP

And God said, "Let there be light"; and there was light.

Daniel 5:11 | AMP

There is a man in your kingdom in whom is a spirit of the holy gods; and in the days of your father, illumination, understanding and wisdom like the wisdom of the gods were found in him. And King Nebuchadnezzar, your father--your father the king, appointed him chief of the magicians, enchanters, Chaldeans and diviners.

Like 11:36 | AMP

So if your whole body is illuminated, with no dark part, it will be entirely bright [with light], as when the lamp gives you light with its bright rays."

Psalms 18:28 | AMP

For You cause my lamp to be lighted and to shine; The Lord my God illumines my darkness.

Proverbs 6:23 | AMP

For the commandment is a lamp, and the teaching [of the law] is light, And reproofs (rebukes) for discipline are the way of life.

John 16:13-16 | NAS

"But when He, the Spirit of truth, comes, He will guide you into all the truth; for He will not speak on His own initiative, but whatever He hears, He will speak; and He will disclose to you what is to come. "He will glorify Me, for He will take of Mine and will disclose it to you. "All things that the Father has are Mine; therefore I said that He takes of Mine and will disclose it to you.

1 Corinthians 4:5 | NAS

Therefore do not go on passing judgment before the time, but wait until the Lord comes who will both bring to light the things hidden in the darkness and disclose the motives of men's hearts; and then each man's praise will come to him from God.

John 14:26 | NAS

"But the Helper, the Holy Spirit, whom the Father will send in My name, He will teach you all things, and bring to your remembrance all that I said to you.

Daniel 5:14 | NAS

"Now I have heard about you that a spirit of the gods is in you, and that illumination, insight and extraordinary wisdom have been found in you.

ENLIGHTENMENT

Psalm 97:11 | NAS

Light is sown like seed for the righteous And gladness for the upright in heart

Daniel 2:22 | NAS

"It is He who reveals the profound and hidden things; He knows what is in the darkness, and the light dwells with Him.

Hebrews 6:4 | NAS

For in the case of those who have once been enlightened and have tasted of the heavenly gift and have been made partakers of the Holy Spirit,

Ephesians 1:18 | NAS

I pray that the eyes of your heart may be enlightened, so that you will know what is the hope of His calling, what are the riches of the glory of His inheritance in the saints,

John 1:9 | NAS

There was the true Light which, coming into the world, enlightens every man.

Hebrews 6:4 | NAS

For in the case of those who have once been enlightened and have tasted of the heavenly gift and have been made partakers of the Holy Spirit,

Psalm 119:130 | NAS

The unfolding of Your words gives light; It gives understanding to the simple.

Psalm 19:8 | NAS

The precepts of the LORD are right, rejoicing the heart; The commandment of the LORD is pure, enlightening the eyes.

Proverbs 6:23 | NAS

For the commandment is a lamp and the teaching is light; And reproofs for discipline are the way of life

ENCOURAGEMENT

Isaiah 35:3 | AMP

Encourage the exhausted, and make staggering knees firm.

1Thessalonians 5:11 | AMP

Therefore encourage and comfort one another and build up one another, just as you are doing.

2 Corinthians 1:4 | AMP

Who comforts and encourages us in every trouble so that we will be able to comfort and encourage those who are in any kind of trouble, with the comfort with which we ourselves are comforted by God.

2 Corinthians 7:6 | AMP

But God, who comforts and encourages the depressed and the disquieted, comforted us by the arrival of Titus.

2 Thessalonians 2:17 | AMP

Comfort and encourage and strengthen your hearts [keeping them steadfast
and on course] in every good work and word.

Hebrews 10:24 | AMP

And let us consider [thoughtfully] how we may encourage one another to
love and to do good deeds,

Proverbs 15:4 | AMP

A soothing tongue [speaking words that build up and encourage] is a tree of
life, but a perversive tongue [speaking words that overwhelm and depress]
crushes the spirit.

2 Corinthians 2:7 | AMP

So instead [of further rebuke, now] you should rather [graciously] forgive
and comfort and encourage him, to keep him from being overwhelmed by
excessive sorrow.

Titus 2:15 | AMP

Tell them these things. Encourage and rebuke with full authority. Let no
one disregard or despise you [conduct yourself and your teaching so as to
command respect].

Colossians 4:8 | AMP

I have sent him to you for this very purpose, that you may know how we
are doing and that he may encourage your hearts;

Deuteronomy 3:28 | AMP

But command Joshua and encourage and strengthen him, for he shall go across and lead this people, and he will give them the land which you see as an inheritance.

2 Samuel 11:25 | AMP

Then David said to the messenger, "Tell Joab this, 'Do not let this thing disturb you, for the sword devours one [side] as well as another. Strengthen your battle against the city and overthrow it'; and so encourage Joab."

Acts 11:23 | AMP

When he arrived and saw the grace of God [that was bestowed on them], he rejoiced and began to encourage them all with an unwavering heart to stay true and devoted to the Lord.

Romans 12:8 | AMP

Or he who encourages, in the act of encouragement; he who gives, with generosity; he who leads, with diligence; he who shows mercy [in caring for others], with cheerfulness.

GLOSSARY

WISDOM:

—noun

the quality or state of being wise; knowledge of what is true or right coupled with just judgment as to action; sagacity, discernment, or insight. scholarly knowledge or learning: wise sayings or teachings; precepts, sense, understanding; sapience, enlightenment

—Synonyms

sense, understanding; sapience, erudition, enlightenment

INSIGHT:

—noun

an instance of apprehending the true nature of a thing, especially through intuitive understanding; penetrating mental vision or discernment; faculty of seeing into inner character or underlying truth;

—Synonyms

perception, apprehension, intuition, understanding, grasp

INSPIRATION:

—noun

an inspiring or animating action or influence; something inspired as an idea

—Synonyms

stimulus, incitement

ILLUMINATION:

—noun

an act or instance of illuminating; intellectual or spiritual enlightenment

—Synonyms

knowledge, revelation, insight, wisdom

ENLIGHTENMENT

—noun

the act of enlightening; the state of being enlightened

—verb (used with object)

to give intellectual or spiritual light to; instruct; impart knowledge to:

to shed light upon; edify, teach, inform

—Synonyms

illumine, edify, teach, inform

ENCOURAGEMENT

—noun

the act of encouraging; the state of being encouraged;

something that encourages

—Synonyms

praise, support, boost, lift, endorsement.

—verb (used with object), en·cour·aged, en·cour·ag·ing

to inspire with courage, spirit, or confidence: to stimulate by assistance, approval, to promote, advance, praise, support, boost, lift, endorsement

—Synonyms

embolden, hearten, reassure; urge; support, aid, help

CONTACT

CEO, DDP Ministries

www.ddpministries.com

Founder, Abundant Reign Ministry Inc., Atlanta, Ga.
www.abundantreignministry.org

Dedric. D Perry may be contacted at ddpministries@yahoo.com for:
Conferences/Revivals/Seminars/Mentorship/Events/Life Coaching/Radio and
TV Interviews

Facebook:

www.facebook.com/DedricD.Perry

www.facebook.com/DDPerryMinistries

fb.me/DedricDPerryCLC

fb.me/DedricDPerryTravels

Twitter @PastaDDP

Instagram @pastadp

WORDS FROM THE AUTHOR

Blessings beloved! I pray that this book has been a tremendous blessing to you! My desire is that all who have read this book would be able to glean from it and receive just what they need. I pray that these wisdom nuggets and simple strategies are applicable to your life, and that they would become a part of your daily living, as they have become a part of mine. My prayer is that much wisdom, insight, inspiration, illumination, enlightenment, and encouragement has been provided. I trust and believe that the impartation that you have received would become a visible manifestation in your life daily, and that it would produce an even greater level of effective living. Remember, we cannot fulfill LIFE until we LIVE LIFE! I would like to conclude with a quote from my husband, Sgt. Anthony F. Perry: "Live is the game, and these are the plays!" #DedricDPerrysPlaybook

God bless and I love you all!

Amen

28870216R00063

Made in the USA
Columbia, SC
18 October 2018